PERCEPTIONS OF EVERYDAY LIFE

CHAD MICHAEL YOUNG

ISBN: 979-8-218-09132-3

Printed in the United States of America

Published by WritersClique.com

"YOU'VE GOT TO LOSE TO
KNOW HOW TO WIN"
AEROSMITH

ABOUT THE BOOK

I have tried to recreate events, locations, and conversations from my memories. In order to maintain their anonymity in some instances I have changed the names of individuals and places. I may have changed some identifying characteristics and details such as physical properties, occupations, and places of residence. If any of the stories contained have any resemblance to persons not to be known by me, living or dead is coincidental.

ACKNOWLEDGMENT

I WANT TO THANK THOUGHS WHO HAVE IMPACTED MY LIFE AND BROUGHT ME TO THE POINT OF WRITING THIS BOOK!

TABLE OF CONTENTS

INTRODUCTION

We all love to hear stories of the rich and famous and all of their excessive behaviors from wild parties, legal problems, divorces, marriages, and on the list can go. I am always amazed at the crazy things people with wealth do. I have been thinking more and more about the average person and why they seem to get lost in the mix, even though they may do crazy things as well. As the world changes, we are starting to hear more and more about the average Joe. With reality television shows and social media, the average person is becoming more prevalent. More and more, it seems that people do not care if their secrets and dirty laundry are exposed for all to see. It is for these reasons I have decided to write about my own experiences.

I want to share my own stories and stories that have been shared with me. Perhaps if an average person such as myself writes a book that others can relate to, they too can realize that it doesn't take millions of dollars to have a good time, you just have to have a good story. You just have to be willing to make yourself vulnerable, open, and honest, and to have some humor when you tell the stories. I hope that the experiences I share will be intriguing enough for people to want to continue reading. Hopefully, you can relate to and enjoy the stories contained herein.

By this premise, I decided to write down events that I have witnessed, or others close to me have witnessed. I have witnessed all the things that make up a memory: sight, sound, smell, touch, and emotions. All this helps shape your mental picture of the memory. What makes us keep reliving certain memories? What causes us to remember certain events? Is it trauma, happiness, sadness, or guilt? Our mind is quite a mystery! As we stumble year by year, day to day, hour by hour, minute by minute through our daily lives we are probably oblivious to our surroundings. Too busy talking on the phone, texting or half-asleep, or possibly just caught in the dry routine of our daily life.

Most people have to make a conscious effort to notice things. This is the reason why there is such a crazy vibe surrounding some people. You know the wacky hairstyles, crazy behavior, everything that can be pierced on a person's body. It is like PLEASE! EVERYONE look at me. Pay attention to me! Flashy, loud, and over the top, mostly, visual stimulants. And the over bathing in cologne. Now, I have an actual problem with detecting how bad or good something really smells. I am guilty myself, of putting on too much cologne. Some people just seem to like to enclose people close to them in a cage of stench and it usually is a scent that is not attractive. PEOPLE, (yes, I'm yelling at you), that musk scented cologne is not a good smell!

I am a person who has tended to stay in the background. I have never really been comfortable being the center of attention. I was shy at a young age, but as an adult I do not feel it's shyness but flying under the radar. It may be a form of wanting to have some control of situations. But it was not always like that! I was not always in control. In fact, I was usually flying blind out of control!

That's enough of my philosophies. Let's get to the stories. I have enjoyed all that has been shared with me and I hope that you enjoy the stories I am choosing to share with you. I hope you even get a good chuckle here or there, even at my expense.

Not everyone can live the life of a celebrity or have the money to do things that will be considered once in a lifetime. Most people live the simple life. So, why has no one told stories from a normal point of view? Are people tired of reading about how the rich live? Most people may perceive a story from a celebrity as spoiled and not the real world. It's time that something was written that an average person could say, I have done that! Or I can do that. Hopefully, you will be able to relate to some of the stories being told. Most of this book was written while sitting in a hotel room. There is not much to do sitting in a room alone except watch TV, gamble online, drink alcohol, something worse I have not thought of, or write about your life. I chose to do the latter.

CHAPTER 1
FIRST MEMORY

The year was about 1975. I was around five years old. I remember riding to a local grocery market named "Genes" that was owned by the Father of someone I would go to school with named Mike and by coincidence, I would work for later in life. It was a grocery store just down the road from my Grandparents house in Chelsea, MI. This was a great store for the people that lived in the area to pick up anything they may need. Meat, vegetables, chips or almost anything you can think of. Local residents would not have to spend the time driving to a bigger city supermarket to get the small items they would need for the week. On this day, my Father Bill and I were in the area of the market and my Father decided he needed something from the store. I don't recall what we were doing out in this area of town. Maybe we were heading see my grandparents who lived just down the road from this store.

My Father pulled his red 1969 Chevrolet pickup truck into the store's gravel parking lot into a parking spot. The dust stirred up by the truck settled on the windshield as my Father shut off the ignition and left the truck's transmission, (which was a column shift) in low, or the bottom position. My Father said, "You wait here, I will only be a minute." At the time, I didn't notice that my Father had left the keys in the ignition. I stayed in the truck and watched through the window as he walked into the store. I was left alone in the truck, because at that time, no one worried about locking doors or even leaving kids in a vehicle. While my Father was in the store, a man dressed in blue overalls opened the driver's side door, got into the driver's seat, and closed the door.

I remember the man had shoulder length, brown scraggily hair. This intruder in the truck, pushed in the clutch, turned the ignition key and tried to start the truck. The truck only turned over, but it didn't start. The truck didn't even sputter. I sat frozen in the passenger seat just looking at the man as he continued trying to get the truck started. After about 20 seconds, the man in blue overalls got fed up. He opened the door, got out of the truck, shut the door, and ran off. I seem to remember that the truck wouldn't start if it were left in the lower transmission position. I remember the same thing happening to my Father. He would try to start the truck in low gear and when it didn't start, he put the shifter up to the park position and then the truck would start. I did not notice where the man in blue overhauls ran off to or even which way he ran. I didn't even really process this moment until many years later. I believe at this point in my life, I was almost kidnapped. The man who attempted to start the truck was probably an escapee from one of the few low-threat level prisons in the area. They always had people simply walking off, because there was no fence surrounding the complex.

Many years later they actually put up fences around the facilities to stop people from walking off. How does a person process an encounter like this? I wonder sometimes, what would have happened to me, if the man in blue overhauls would have got the vehicle started. Would he have shoved me out and stole the truck, or would he have taken off with me in the vehicle and taken me to a location of his choosing to do something criminal to me. It's scary to think what may have been the outcome. There is the possibility that I would not be here writing about this today. Maybe a convict out there remembers the encounter.

As far back as this happened, I still remember it like it happened today. I still remember the orange C-10 Chevy pickup too. This may be the reason that brought me to write about my life. Maybe I was spared during this time for a greater purpose. Maybe I was selected to let people know that you don't have to be rich and famous to know that you have a purpose in this life. Maybe my purpose, while living what I consider an average life, is to write about it, to show others that while you may think you have an average life is actually very interesting to others and to write about it and keep a record for your family or for others.

CHAPTER 2
EARLY ON...TROUBLE MAKER

Some people are rowdy in their younger years, which can continue through adulthood. But it usually starts in our youth. Children can be very energetic, which can lead them to mischievous behaviors. They can become bored when they are not stimulated or challenged intellectually. Certainly, this is the case with some child stars. Sometimes they are exposed to adult situations they don't understand. With their fame comes money and exposure to adult situations. I certainly remember that there were plenty of kids labeled "bad" in school growing up. Not doing the work, skipping class, showing up late, and mouthing off to the teachers are just a few examples. But what are the reasons? Is it bad parenting? The wrong crowds they are hanging out with, too much idle time on their hands? Maybe the person is just a bad seed? Nowadays, everything is blamed on Attention Deficit Disorder or A.D.D. I think this is the case in many situations.

I look back when I was younger and I remember having a lot of energy and I was a challenge to my parents, Bill and Carol Young and I was also a bit of a hell-raiser. I never got into a lot of trouble that I recall, maybe that is because I did not commit horrible and terrible things or perhaps, I just didn't get caught! I remember not getting in trouble in school, when there were a few schoolmates that were always causing trouble and instigating others to participate in their devious behaviors that seemed to be spending time in detention. I only spent one time in detention and I don't remember what it was for. I do remember that there were the "usual" people there. The people that skipped school, that were tardy, or didn't follow other simple school related rules. People that seemed to do more things that some would consider "wrong" outside of school.

Very early in elementary school, when I was in fourth or fifth grade, they had a program that tried to teach the children responsibility by allowing older kids to volunteer to be on a safety patrol. If you signed up and were chosen, you would be presented with the task of walking children home that were a few years younger than you. You had to make sure that the sidewalk was clear of obstacles and make sure that all of the road crossings were safe of vehicles and the sort. So, the school was enlisting kids to put younger children's lives in their hands! This was a great task I concluded. You got to get out of class to watch a few younger children for a little while.

One of the times I did this task, I remember walking a couple of children home who lived close to the elementary school. We got to the first kid's house without any sort of problem but upon reaching the second child's home, he realized he had lost some belongings. Some drawings that he felt were priceless works of art that he created in art class. I said, "They are long gone by now." "The wind has taken them away." The child got a tear in his eye and ran into his home. I proceeded back to the school and I thought to myself as I started walking back, "Stupid kid should have held onto them!" A couple blocks back towards the school, I saw the papers laying on the sidewalk, almost presenting themselves to me to grab up and run back to the home where the sad child was professing his sadness about them to his Mother by now. I kicked them out of my path as I continued walking and muttered something like, "Dumb kid should have had a better grip!" I think I still have the same attitude now. I really don't feel bad about this now. The child probably learned to have a tighter grip on the things he loved. I may have taught him a good lesson!

On occasion, I would stay with my Father's sister Vesta when she lived in Ann Arbor, and her son Mike and I would venture around the neighborhood. Occasionally, my cousin, Mike's Sister Rhonda would join us. I was probably eight to twelve years old at the time. Mike and I, and occasionally Mike's sister Rhonda, would walk through the neighborhood, and sometimes would go up to the local "Quick Pick," which was a connivance store. This area was a "ruff" area even back in the day. There were unsavory characters here and there. But I was with my cousin Mike, who was either my age or a tad older, and he "knew" the area and also knew people around the neighborhood, so we never felt in any danger.

We were walking home, back to my Aunt's house after getting a pop and or candy from the store and just going for a walk. This meant walking along the row of houses in the subdivision on the sidewalk. And most of the houses had fenced-in yards. One of the houses we were walking by, which also had a chain-link fenced around the yard, had a dog in the front yard. It was a Doberman. The dog was just walking along near the fence, close to where we were, and seemed to be walking along with us as we walked by. The dog was just minding its business, sniffing the ground, not really paying attention to us, but still keeping up with us. I looked over at the dog, as we continued our walk and said in a normal child's hi-pitched voice, "Hi doggie". The dog proceeded to jump right up on the chain link fence with its two front paws dangling over the top of the fence and barked at me with the most terrorizing bark you can imagine, as if saying, "Don't you DARE speak a word to me." I probably jumped back ten feet towards the road. Of course, in normal fashion, my cousin, and his sister burst out in laughter. You may not think this is that great of a story, but it shows that we all enjoy laughing at our misfortunes. We tend to do this as children and even as adults.

Another memory that occurred to me was the time I was in Junior high and there was yet again another program in place to promote responsibility in youth. You could sign up to be a referee in the Special Olympics. Myself and a friend at the time, a person who went on to spend a number of years of his adult life in prison, decided that a great way to get out of going to class was to volunteer for this activity. So, we were picked and we joined these special people out on the field for the games. To us, it was just a way to get out of class. At the time, I suppose I looked down on these individuals I was around, but after a while I believe I saw a lot of determination from these kids. I don't know if I realized it at the time, I was there being the referee, but looking back now I have the utmost respect for these people. They don't let their handicap stop them from achieving their goals. Many of us should look upon them for our inspiration for the very same thing we are looking for out of life.

My memories of my Paternal Grandfather are funny to me, because the first thought is always my cousins and I running around my Grandparent's house up North. Running down to the basement, running around the basement, then running back upstairs, and out into the living room, then back downstairs. And the whole time this is going on, we are laughing and probably screaming. The thunder of our feet echoed on the floors as we went room to room. When we got around the dining room table, where my Paternal Grandfather was sitting, he could not take it anymore and would scold us doing a half yell. Not yelling, but not talking softly either.

He would say loudly "HEY, HEY, HEY, HEY" at which point we would stop, or slow down and get quiet. My Grandmother would say, "You guys need to go somewhere else." And then we probably would go back downstairs and start the process again. I probably gained a great respect for my Paternal Grandfather, when he gave me a clock for my graduation; he made it for my graduation present in 1988 from a cut of a tree. I still have the clock to this day and it still works. There is nothing like a quality, hand made present! It was not until much, much later in life, probably when I was in my twenties, that I fully understood my Grandfather. I do not know how he put up with us kids. If it had been me, I would have knocked some heads! He acted tough, but he had a great heart, and loved his Grandchildren. No matter how much we irritated him!

A fairly tame child you may be thinking? I guess I was at first when very young, but I became a little more devious as I started to get older. While on a vacation with the family up north when my cousin and I were about ten or eleven and we were visiting our Paternal Grandparents. One of our younger cousins, who we rarely saw, was about age six or seven was also attending the visit. Of course, our parents forced my cousin Mike and myself, to let the younger cousin hang out and play with us. So, we came up with the deduction that if we were going to be forced to do this, then we would put him through a series of tests. An initiation so to speak. So, my cousin and I went out beforehand and scouted some good obstacles and things for the younger cousin to go through. There was a creek that snaked throughout the woods behind my Grandparents house and we found some nice spots for some tests for him to do.

So, after we scouted and set up a few things we took the younger cousin out with us. I told him with an evil voice, "If you want to be in our club, you must pass a few tests first. Just down from my Grandparents house, where the creek crossed under the road, there was an exceptionally large drain that run under the road and it was big enough to walk through. Even though there was water flowing through the drain, it wasn't deep enough to really get your shoes waterlogged. We walked along with this young man and led him down the road and into the drain under the road. As we were walking in, we made ghostly sounds that echoed off the metal just to help set the mood. We proceeded to stop in the middle of the drain. Standing there silent with the water flowing past us in the drain and echoing off the walls, a kind of eerie feeling comes over you. The flowing water at times getting drops of water on the tops of our shoes. It is a fairly long drain and probably seemed very long to children.

My cousin told the younger cousin, "The first test is the drain of death." (All of the tests had names that we came up with, probably on the spot), you have to stand here, at this exact spot for at least 5 minutes and you can't move". The younger cousin said with high confidence, "I can do that." My older cousin said, "Ok, we are going to go to the other end of the drain and wait just out of site. Then we will let you know when 5 minutes has passed and you can come out." "Ok," my younger cousin said.

My cousin and I started walking out of the drain. As we made our way out of the lonely cylinder, with the sound of water echoing off its sides, and the water flowing past the younger boy's shoes, my older cousin turned around and said, "Don't let the piranhas get you." "What?" my younger cousin replied as the confidence was now draining from him. "Don't let the piranhas get you." My older cousin seemed to sneer again. This is Northern Michigan. Of course, there are no piranhas in Michigan, but my younger cousin did not know that. After we left the drain, we were just out of sight, but still talking to him. "Still doing ok in there?" one of us asked. "Yes," a weak voice responded from the inside of the drain. My older cousin said, "Hey, I think I just saw a piranha swim into the drain going your way!" All of a sudden, the younger cousin let out a scream that was amplified about ten times because of the metal in the drain.

The young child came sprinting out of the tunnel with terror in his eyes. He joined us on the outside of the drain with a look on his face that he just faced certain death! "That was a close call" I told the youngster as he stood there out of breath. We led the young man on to his next challenge. This one was called "The River of Death." (All of the challenges seemed to have the word death in them) This was strange; because it was a creek that was probably ankle to knee deep. There may have been some trout in the creek, but that was about it.

We told the young man for this test, he had to try to jump across the creek without falling in the water. Of course, we picked the largest spot, so that there was no way he was going to be able to do it. My older cousin added, "If you do fall in, hurry up and get out as soon as you can, because the piranhas are usually hungry this time of day." My cousin, Mike, and I both jumped over the creek with ease, because of our age and the long legs we both had. We knew because he was so short, he would not be able to jump across.

One of us said to the younger cousin, "Ok, this should be easy for you." With absolute determination, the young cousin rocked back and forth and gave it his all. And he failed miserably. His head was about the only thing that landed on shore. I wildly yelled, "Hurry up and get out, they are coming!" It looked like fast motion as his legs scurried back and forth, not being able to get any traction on the slippery clay bank of the creek. We finally extended a hand and helped him out of the water. "Man, you have had a couple of close calls." My older cousin said.

We arrived at the last of the challenges. The dreaded "Bridge of Death." Earlier, we had placed some branches over the creek to cross over to the other side. But we cracked one of the main branches almost in half and put it back together, so that if you stepped on it, you would break it and fall into the creek. We told the young challenger, "Pass this test and you have made it into the group." We had him go first and we reminded him that he was lucky so far to escape the razor-sharp teeth of the piranha in the water. He approached the sticks that covered the creek and probably took one step into the middle of them and of course they broke, and he went right into the water. "Hurry up and get out of there!" my older cousin yelled.

The frightened young man in the water was trying to escape, but he kept losing his balance because the rocks under the water at the bottom of the creek were slippery. "There is one eating on your leg!" I shrieked. And with that, he managed to get out of the water. We joined the dripping wet and freighted younger cousin on the other side of the creek after crossing the wooden bridge. We told him there was really no piranha in the creek and that it had all been for fun. The angered little man was not pleased to hear this. He proceeded to march into my Grandma and Grandpa's house and told everyone what my cousin and I had put him through. I do not remember getting in any trouble because of this, although his Mother, my Aunt was very angry with us!

One of the early memories I have of my Maternal Grandfather, is when he was talking about the chickens he had. He gave them all names. The main two I remember are Chicken George, a big, all white rooster that was the leader of the pack and Quentin, a black rooster that was smaller, with red on his feathers. He said that they would walk around his house continuously all day long! My Grandfather was very amused at how you could watch the chickens slowly walk and peck the ground as they walk going around the house all day. He said if you got too close to the group of chickens, Chicken George would attack you.

My Grandfather would add to the story at this point by flapping his arms as if he had wings, to show what the rooster did to his predators. One fine sunny day, our family went over to see Grandpa and Grandma Hughes (as we always called them). It must have been about 1977. We all got out of the car and immediately noticed that the chickens were in close proximity to where we were. My sister Laurel, who is three years younger than me and probably, was about four years old at the time, thought she would walk over to the chickens to inspect what they were doing. Chicken George suddenly took charge to protect the pack and flew up into my sister Laurel's face, violently flapping his wings. Laurel ran from the incident, crying and in a total state of fear. My Grandfather came out of his house and in a rage chased the chickens away. He would not stand for his grandchildren being attacked. I think soon after this, he got rid of them.

About 4th grade, I remember a couple of things that luckily didn't happen to me, or they may be something that would still haunt me to this day. There was an individual that was picked on a lot because he was rather slow and dim witted named "Marvin". He didn't deserve it, but he still got picked on plenty.

I walked into the boy's bathroom at the elementary school to find this poor fellow dumping water out of his boot into the toilet. He obviously had his boot forcibly taken off and thrown into the toilet. I don't remember laughing or feeling sympathy at the time, but I should have.

I also remember Marvin, around the same time had stepped in a big piece of dog feces. A group of kids stood there and laughed at Marvin as he scraped it off on the sidewalk just outside of the school and then simply walked away like it wasn't even phasing him. He left behind a four to five foot long track of dog feces on the sidewalk. It stayed there it seemed for months, through all the rain and wind and eventually it started to become less noticeable until it was finally gone completely.

Marvin did not exactly help himself. I recall a time during class at the same school where I needed to use the restroom. After getting permission from the teacher, I left the class and made my way to the bathroom. Once in there, I walked next to the stalls and Marvin jumped down from within one of the stalls yelling, "Raaa" I was very startled. He laughed hysterically and he said, "I got you," while pointing at me with his pleasure. I said, "Yea, I guess so." I left thinking, why was Marvin hanging out in the bathroom waiting for someone to scare while he should have been in class learning? I should have felt sorry for what this poor fellow went through in his younger years. If I remember these things now and they didn't even happen to me, I wonder if the person they happened to remembers them. It would haunt me, I think. I think that some people are affected for life from the things that happen to them as a child. I still remember things that happened to me in Elementary, Middle, and High School.

While in the fourth grade, a few people decided to play a game where you look into a mirror in the bathroom, with the lights off, while saying a phrase such as "Mother Mary Forgive Me" three times and you were supposed to see a witch's reflection in the mirror. I walked into the boy's bathroom with one or two other people, not expecting to see anything because I didn't believe it. I turned off the light and religiously said the phrase softly, "Mother Mary Forgive Me," then slightly louder, "Mother Mary Forgive Me," then quite loud, "Mother Mary Forgive Me." And looked in the mirror, just then I saw a flash of something in the mirror. A face we thought.

It was somewhat light all of a sudden in the bathroom with the lights off. I was so scared I ran towards the door of the bathroom. As I slammed my body against the door, I heard a moan of agony. I found out later, the face and light we saw in the mirror was the teacher of the class I was supposed to be in, coming into the bathroom to check on what the commotion was. She unfortunately pushed open the door and put her hand inside the doorway as she pushed it open to investigate what the ruckus was that was going on in the boy's bathroom. And as I slammed against the door in fear, it shut completely closed and it broke her hand. I remember walking out of the bathroom and watching the teacher walking down the hallway holding her hand. The following year, the same teacher did not have any of the same students in any of her classes the following year, except one person, I think. And this person never really said a word so that's probably why they had the teacher again the next year for 5th grade. I guess I wouldn't blame her.

That is not the only time I broke a bone in someone else's body. I think I was in about ninth grade in high school gym playing racquetball with a friend of mine and the game of ours was getting heated. The usual taunts and yelling that go along with the competitive part of any sport was also in full play. I yelled at the top of my lungs, "Miss it wuss!" while my opponent would respond, "You can't hit the side of a barn."

As we continued the hot game and the ball was coming back at us as hard as we were hitting it. My friend hit the ball towards the wall and I went for the rebound. As the ball bounced back, I wound up, slammed a shot and hit the ball as hard as I could and I hit my friend's hand, because he was standing too close to me in the process. He kind of jumped up and down shaking his hand in a most unpleasant agony uttering profanities. I think my first response was to point at him and laugh at how stupid he looked jumping up and down. He even informed the gym teacher that there might be a problem because his hand was in excruciating pain. The gym teachers simply looked at him with a "Get over it" look and declared that maybe he should go put some ice on it.

I later found out that I indeed had broken his hand. I don't remember playing racquetball again after that. Maybe the school deemed it as too dangerous! I seemed to have a knack for hurting other people and not even trying to. At the time, I may have even had the attitude, "Hey, look what I did!"

CHAPTER 3
WHOLESOME TIME IN CHURCH...

Some people attend church and some people don't. I believe everyone is entitled to worship or not worship religion, as they want. I do believe that if you attend church as a child, it will most likely instill morals and a common belief of goodness that will follow you on to your adult life. I suppose if a strenuous view is placed upon someone as a child, it can damage an individual over time, just as not having a viewpoint placed at all. Probably the best way to tell is to instill what teachings you choose on your child and hope for the best!

I went to a Methodist church from a very young age. I believe everyone should probably go to some kind of church as a child to help instill good morals and values within the child to shape them for the person they will grow up to be. I think it was a very good experience for me, as I remember many of the things I was taught to this day. I remember the people that taught the lessons as well as the lessons they taught. I also have many wonderful remembrances of people who went to the church. I also recall a lot of funerals. There happened to be a lot of older people in the congregation of the church. I still remember many of the older faces that belonged to the church. Sadly, most of them, if not all, are gone now. That's why pictures are so essential. So, you never forget.

People are remembered in death as they were in life. No matter how well the Mortician dresses them and does them up with makeup. A good example is one of the congregation members that I knew growing up that went to the church. He was a farmer by trade and had toiled out in the fields, probably all of his life. The farmer worked at the local feed and farm store. He always had a long unkempt beard and dirt under his fingernails, but he would at least wear clean clothes when he went to church. So, I guess being somewhat clean when attending church was important to him. When he died, we went to his viewing and my uncle Jeff remarked, "He never looked this clean in real life." And it was true. But I guess when you die and are buried; you get to look good even if you didn't in everyday life.

Don't think for a second that just because I was in church, I was not still being a rowdy child. Another child in the church that was the same age as me, about five or six at the time that I would grow up with, seemed to also have this mischief streak in him. We would make paper airplanes and at the end of the church service when the people were getting up to leave, we would throw them in the air and watch them soar through the church. The paper airplanes seemed to soar oh so high. Almost like a greater force was pushing them up as high as they could possibly go!

At some point the short organist that played the hymns for the church grabbed us both by the shirt and seemed to sneer in her hi pitched voice "That isn't a good thing to be doing in the church," so we stopped. Another thing I enjoyed doing, either before service or after service was to pull myself along under the rows of pews. There was a very smooth hardwood floor in the church, so you could slide along underneath the pews to the front of the row, turn around and slide back. You could lay on your back and pull yourself along or lay on your stomach and use your feet to push yourself through! I don't know why this was so fun but I remember doing it.

The church had a Halloween theme during the month of October, which was very enjoyable. They had bobbing for apples, best costume contest, donuts, cider, and also a hayride. Every year a local farmer who lived just a couple houses down from my Mom and Dad would load a wagon up with hay, everyone would get in at the church and he would drive us around the block. It seemed like it was about an hour ride. It was fun for both kids and adults. I always looked forward to it. These sorts of things happened every October for years.

As I started to grow a little older, the same old things seemed to get boring. I suggested we do a new attraction. A graveyard maze. And somehow the "Elders" of the church gave it approval. We ran a rope, starting at the front of the church, through the large church graveyard, winding through the different parts and grave stones, way to the back of the property and then back to the front. People would hold onto the rope and follow along the route winding through the graveyard, until you came back out the front. Doesn't sound too scary.

But when you add it was done at night and we had people stationed along the way to jump out in costumes and scare people, it turned out to be very scary. Of course, I had to spice it up. When we were laying out the maze during the day and putting up the rope, I saw a snake and someone went and killed it. So, I draped the dead snake over the rope, so the first person through the maze would walk along, holding the rope and eventually the persons hand would run into the snake draped over the rope. I don't know if the snake ever scared anyone because as soon as the maze opened and the first group went through, there was so much screaming going on.

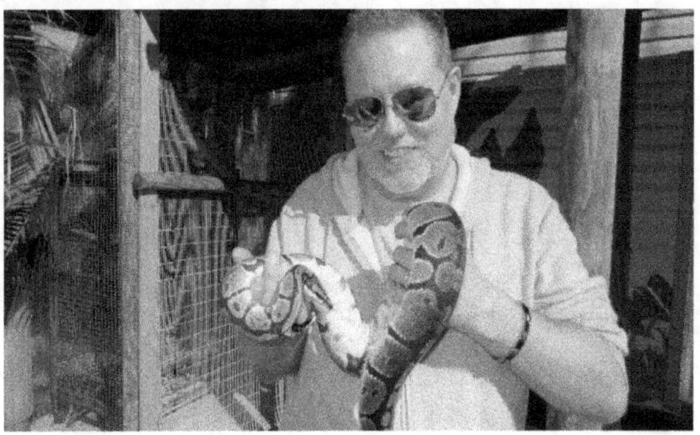

With all of the actors popping out during the maze, scaring people and the fact that the patrons were walking through a graveyard, it was hard to tell what was scaring them. It was just total confusion. Little kids were so scared they were running for the front of the church. People were tripping and falling over the smaller headstones that you couldn't see in the dark. I don't know if anyone even made it through the maze to the end. In any event, that was the first and last time we did the haunted maze for Halloween at the church.

As part of living in a neighborhood with a church, during the warm months of the year, a lot of the kids would ride their bicycles down to the church. If you rode up to the Highway overpass, located just up the road a few hundred feet from the church, you could ride down the road and get going very fast by the time you got to the church. This was a paved road that ran on an incline down in front of the church, so you could go pretty fast. A bunch of us kids would ride up to the bridge that crossed over an expressway and then ride down. You could get going so fast and then just coast past the church down to the end of the road. Yes, it might sound boring, but that is what us country kids did!

One of the times, a local kid that went to the church had just got a new bicycle and it was a nice looking bike. I talked him into letting me ride it. I rode up to the top of the bridge overpass and turned around and positioned myself for the ride back down. I was going to ride down as fast as I could go. So, as the other children looked on, I placed my foot on the pedal and started down the hill. I pedaled so fast I had to be breaking a speed record I thought. As I rode past the church in a blur to most of the spectators, I decided I had went far enough and decided I needed to brake. Unfortunately, I pressed the wrong handle, since I was used to the brakes on my own bicycle and which one controlled which wheel. I had pressed the front brake handle. The bicycle seemed to freeze in time, as I went right over the handlebars and broke the fall with my right hand as I toppled over end over end. As I got up from my "accident," I tried to stay as composed as possible, because the neighborhood children were looking on. I got up and assessed the damage to the bike, which seemed to be minimal. I walked the bike over to the owner and said sorry, it didn't damage it, now knowing if it really had. I walked over to the church front steps and sat down. I looked over the damages to myself and noticed blood running from my wrist. I had scraped a layer of skin from my wrist, but that was really the extent of it. I kind of played it out like I planned it. "Did you like my trick?" I asked. I don't think anyone believed it. The wound on my wrist continued to get infected and bleed in the coming days. I continued to treat it with peroxide and Band-Aids and it finally stopped bleeding. I still have the scar from this incident to this day.

One day an older, married couple from the church told me they had an "old fashioned car" probably a car from the thirties, that they drove in the Chelsea Fourth of July parade each year and they asked if I would like to ride with them in the parade. Being around eight or ten years old at the time and up to this point had only participated in a parade by watching the parade go by, I jumped at the chance. And as luck would have it, my sister Laurel, my cousin Mike and his sister Rhonda were also there at the time, so of course, this nice older couple asked them too.

So, when the 4th of July came, all four of us got to ride in the rumble seat of this car in the fourth of July parade in Chelsea, Michigan! What's really so great about that you ask? Well, that's not the reason for writing this. As you know, normally with a parade, the people in the parade throw out candy to the spectators who are watching. Usually, kids run and pick up the candy. So here we are, the four of us kids in the rumble seat and the couple who owned the car were sitting in the front riding along the slowly moving parade route. We all waved to the people, watching as we drove along at snails pace. We had the candy to throw out from where we were sitting, in the rumble seat, which we did. But after a while, we grew tired and bored of this. Tossing candy out to people really wasn't much fun to us. I don't remember who devised the plan, but apparently some or all of us started really pelting the kids with the candy.

Trying to hit kids in the head that were just standing there watching seemed like more fun! This only seemed to hold our attention for a little bit. The kids seemed oblivious that the candy was coming at them like a fastball. So, we took things a step further. Someone, my older cousin Mike or myself, we don't remember who, decided we should eat the candy ourselves and replace the now empty candy wrapper with the small pebbles located from the small pebble quarry located at our feet on the vehicle's floorboards! All of us seemed to get such satisfaction out of throwing the now pebble filled candy wrappers out to the kids. I'm sure some unfortunate children opened the candy to feast on the sugary delight, only to be greeted by a small stone. They must have looked dumb founded as they stared at it, wondering why there was a rock instead of candy. I don't remember if we ever got caught doing this, but the memory sure is caught in my head!

What I most remember about church, are the morals that were instilled into my soul. They were not forced onto me. It had to be the stories that were gently induced into me! I do not want to steal from people. I don't want to kill people. I value the bond of my marriage. When we are young, we obviously don't care about much and that is why things have to be beaten into our brains sometimes! So, we remember as Adults. And when we do indeed become adults, hopefully, we have retained some of the things we learned as children to help guide us through our journey along the rocky road of life.

CHAPTER 4
VACATIONS WITH THE FAMILY

Almost everyone can relate to vacations with their family. All the good memories, as well as the bad. From being crammed in a car, to even riding in a plane to get to the destination. This is the structure that people will most likely continue into the adult life. If you have children, and you are not a wealthy person you will most likely travel with the family in a car if you go on a vacation. I currently do all traveling by airplane, which is opposite of what I experienced as a child. My parents would drive us to our vacation spots. I like to get to a destination in the shortest amount of time. That way, you have more time to enjoy the vacation itself, so I have always flown since I have been an adult when I travel, unless it was an hour or two away, in which case, why would you waste the money on a plane?

My parents took our family on many vacations as a child. I remember quite a lot of them. While on one vacation, the family stopped in an area that had a beach. This area was very muddy. My brother Kent was about three or four and sped out to the beach, away from where we were, to catch the waves. He stepped into the muddy shoreline and all of a sudden we heard him crying. We came closer to the area where he was and all he kept saying was, "It's gone," "It's gone," "It's gone." My Mother asked, "What's gone." Kent screamed, "My shoe, it's gone." He had stepped in the mud and when his foot pulled up, the shoe was not on his foot. The mud had swallowed it up! I don't think we ever got it back.

I remember my Father started doing something like what I'm doing now. Writing down the stories of the trips we took together. Taking down on paper the things that happened day to day. The members of our family that may read this can remember staying at the campground where Yogi Bear showed up waving to the kids in the campground. The park ranger showed up, loaded Yogi up in his Jeep and took off with him to wherever he was taking him. My brother Kent who was probably 4 years old at the time began waving into the air while screaming, "Goodbye Yogi, goodbye Yogi," until the screaming turned into crying, "Goodbye Yogi, goodbye Yogi," I remember it all. I was there, and now you are too. Yes, we all have many stories like this that happened while we were on vacation when we were younger.

I was not always a good boy out on a family vacation. I recall staying at a campground that had campground restrooms. Maybe it was a family style restroom back then where both sexes could go in. I seem to remember my sister Laurel was with me on this excursion. For some reason, in this bathroom, it seemed to me to be the best time in the whole world to take some toilet paper, a whole handful of it, wet it under a stream of running water and throw it at the bathroom wall. I had never done this before. I don't know what made me think of doing it and I don't think I have ever done it since this time. But during the stay at this campground with my family it was certainly a task that was fulfilled.

I would grab some toilet paper, run it under water, then throw it at the wall in the bathroom and watch it splatter and stick to the wall. I'm sure I got my sister Laurel to partake in the event also! I did this quite a few times before I got tired of it and left. Later, I went back to the bathroom and found a little old lady cleaning the toilet paper off of the wall. I sort of felt sorry for the old lady, having caused her this major job that she seemed to be employed to have to do. As she was scraping the now dried toilet paper chunks off the wall, she noticed my sister Laurel and myself as we walked into the bathroom. She turned and said very angrily, "Do you guys know who did this?" I replied with a concerned tone "No, but I hope you find the person who did it. What kind of an animal would do such a thing?" After I got out of the "hot zone." I laughed to myself at my mis-deed. Now of course, if the shoe were on the other foot, I would be livid if I had to clean up some snot nose punks mess!

As a young child, I also spent a lot of my time with family I did not see all of the time. I am glad I had these experiences as I look back on it now, and I am more appreciative of having all the wonderful memories! Our family spent a lot of time with immediate relatives. Going to their house, going up North, or going to family reunions, which as I remember, used to be exclusively on my Father's side of the family. Family reunions used to be very important to my great Aunt and Grandmother. It seemed to be a very important event that we, as a family, would look forward to. We visited with all of the relatives who primarily lived in the northern part of Lower Michigan. In attendance would be my Great Aunt Vesta and Uncle Jerry who owned a cherry orchard, along with their kids, Dwight, Carol and Nancy. My Aunt Josie and her daughter Yvonne, and of course Grandpa and Grandma Young! We would all get together and my Paternal Grandfather would make his home made ice cream. It was an old hand-crank maker, so when he would get tired, he would make all us kids take a turn cranking. If anyone started whining, he would say, "If you don't want to crank it, you won't get any ice cream!" So, we all would suck it up and crank the machine. I don't think anyone had to worry about not getting any of the cold, frozen treat if they didn't crank the ice cream maker. That was just a "motivator"! It was always a joy and pleasure to see the extended family up North.

I would also spend time at my maternal Grandparent's home, which was about 10 miles from my parent's house. When I was young, I would stay overnight at my grandparents' house. I remember a few times staying with them, for a day or two (probably to give my parents a break from ME!). At the time, my uncle (my Mother's youngest brother) was still living with my Grandparents. He worked at the Ann Arbor Airport. Out in front of my Grandparent's house, there was a field. It probably wasn't that large of a field, but through a child's eyes, it looked huge.

Looking at it, with a child's imagination, it was an airstrip where planes take off and land. My Grandmother and myself were outside in the front of the house. I do not remember what we were doing at the time, but I remember saying, "Too bad Uncle Jeff didn't have an airplane; he could take off and fly to work." My Grandmother replied very reassured, "Don't you worry, he flies to work in his car!" At the time, I may not have really understand the comment, but now, every time I think about it, it gives me a chuckle.

Another memory I have when I was about the same age, another uncle of mine was in the process of building his first retirement home. My Uncle Mike and Aunt Sheila built the business from the ground up and it was a business my Aunt and

Uncle would run for 33 years, until they retired. I remember when the building was completed, and my family went up to see it. The inside was painted and all the trim work was done and the carpet was installed. There were still some construction workers on the site, finishing up some remaining work. My sister and I were running around from room to room, playing. We had a field day.

In this huge building, with many patients rooms all empty of furniture. A different type of playground, but still a playground to us kids! One of the workers said, "Hey, you kids shouldn't be here!" I responded in a manner as though I was royalty. With my hands on my hips, I said in a very condescending tone, "My uncle owns this place, so I can do what I want!" Pretty firm for a child of eight to ten if I do say so myself!

Everyone grows up eventually. Sometimes it just takes longer for some. But it seems nowadays, some people never seem to grow up. People are cuddled by their parents for most of their adult life and never take responsibility for anything. Growing up as a child, if we ever got caught doing any of the many things that we did, we would have had to endure the repercussions. We would have to pay some kind of restitution. We would be forced to take responsibility for our actions. This is part of the problem today. There is no responsibility for actions. Kids seem to be the adults in the family, making adult decisions and the parents don't do anything about it. Part of the downfall of society, I guess. I say let all people take responsibility for their actions. Adults are responsible for their kids and adults are only responsible for themselves. Why should I have to pay for someone that has made bad decisions, while I have made responsible decisions? Enjoy your childhood people, because once it is gone, life only gets harder!

CHAPTER 5
PEOPLE WATCHING

We all look at other people, whether we want to or not. It can at times be rather entertaining and it can also make us feel better about ourselves! It can happen at your place of employment or at a bar or restaurant. It may simply be as you are walking on the street or even at home. This can make us feel many different emotions. Maybe anger if someone wears something offensive. Happiness or joy if the person is just jumping around and perhaps singing and dancing, which may make us laugh. Or maybe sadness if we happened to see a funeral persuasion. I think everyone reacts differently to the different things they see people do and say.

But actual "people watching" is a personal past time of mine. When we are on vacation, we like to sit out in a warm climate, maybe at a bar or restaurant where you can sit outside to watch the different types of people walking by. Looking at the way they dress, the way they act, and the things they are talking about. It always sickens me when you are out in public and people are walking around in their pajamas. Whether it is at a grocery store, a mall or any place for that matter. You are not at home. You are in public! Put on clothes. I do not know how many times we have been out getting groceries and the people we see, look like they have rolled out of bed, grabbed the car keys, and went out. It is mostly the women. Their hair up in the bun, and their skuzzy, frizzy hair that seems to poke your eyeballs with its long strands sticking out. They either have pajamas or sweats on.

Yes folks, it is not a good look. People who do this are pretty much perceived by the public as lazy. Why would anyone want to be thought of as this? They just do not seem to care. Now, if you walk out to your mailbox to get the mail like this, hey, it is your property. Go in the nude if you want, although, the police may have a word with you. It seems people don't have much class anymore. It is a different world. Some do not care what they look or unfortunately smell like.

Have you ever been next to someone that has not bathed on a hot summer day? B.O. is in full display! How about having to be stuck sitting next to an individual like this for a seminar or something similar? Please my friends, pay attention to your hygiene!

My brother in law Kevin, I believe does a lot of people watching! He is in my opinion a great storyteller and has enlightened the family with his many stories about the people he has seen or had encounters with. He always seems to remember the slightest details about people and I believe it really makes the story interesting. At least in my opinion. He could probably write his own book! Hearing someone like this describe what they see and encounter probably leaves an unconscious state in your mind on what you need to recreate the setting and circumstance when retelling something you have seen.

I tend to make people watching into a game at times or simply look at the spectacle before me. My wife and I or whomever I may be with, like to play a sort of game sometimes when we are out and people watching. We like to say, hey that person looks like Burt Reynolds, Owen Wilson, Courtney Love. You get the picture. Being mistaken for Burt Reynolds, in my opinion would be cool. I would love to be mistaken for Burt Reynolds. At a bar, we were playing the game, I saw a Julia Louis-Dreyfus look alike, a Billy Bob Thorton, and David Schwimmer look alike. The guy looked so much like David Schwimmer, I felt compelled to tell him so. With music that was being played feeding my ears, I walked out on the dance floor where the impersonator was dancing with a lovely lady. I walked up to him with the confidence of the president of the United States, tapped him on the shoulder and loudly said to him, "Hey, do you know you look like David Scwhimmer from the television show Friends?" He turned to me and pointed to his shirt, which said, "I'm not Ross from Friends."

We both proceeded to laugh hysterically, and then we continued to talk after the song that was playing was over. I was playing in a local band that night at this establishment, so he recognized me and wanted to hang out and buy me a drink. So, by me going to him, and making a simple observation, he in turn found me to be just as interesting. It is funny how people think. Over the years, I played in many different bands and I never felt like a celebrity. I guess I was never that crass, or egotistical. Although, some of the other people in the band I played with were just that.

As I have said, when I am on vacation, I like to sit outside and watch the various people of the cities I am visiting, go by. They are going to wherever they may be going. Some are simply residents that are going to or coming home from working for the day. Others are possibly tourists. They come in all shapes and sizes. Dressed in all different kinds of outfits. Some are dressed very nice, others, let us say, are dressed with such a small amount of material that should never be stretched over so much "body."

People watching does not necessarily mean just standing back in a crowd and watching the people walking by and making observations, it can also mean waiting and watching as people walk by to initiate a confrontation of some sort with the person.

One of the places I worked at when I was younger was The Methodist Retirement Home, in Chelsea, MI. We worked in the dietary department and it was a fairly good job. It did not pay really well, but it was a great "starter" job. A great way for a teenager to learn the task of earning and hopefully saving money. Hopefully that is. I was always good at saving money. I never spent beyond my means and I didn't like to owe money to anyone. I met lots of people and made a lot of friends working at the retirement home, a lot of whom I am still friends with today on social media. I have quite a few stories from working here.

This certain story is about my friend at the time that also worked at the retirement home. He went into the refrigerated cooler where they kept the milk and other goods that needed to be kept cold. There was a shelf where they kept the milk, that was about 1 ½' – 2' off the ground. And the crates of milk would be stacked up on this shelf. There was just enough room to hide under the shelf. And my friend did just that. He would lay on the floor, in the cooler, under the milk shelf, and wait for girls to come into the cooler, then he would grab at their legs and listen to them scream out in fear. So, he watched people (mostly girls) come in the cooler and then scared them! I'm sure there was some sort of gratification by grabbing and scaring the girls and making them scream out of fear. But I never thought of that at the time, but looking back at this individual during that time, I would not have been surprised if some sort of sick satisfaction was achieved by doing this.

You may be people watching at times and not even realize it. Things happen when you least expect it. I went to a rock concert in 1996 to see Robert Plant and Jimmy Page, a couple of old rock icons. It was a great concert. But the main part that I will never forget is what happened to a guy at the concert. I like to sit and just watch concerts. Others prefer to stand up at the excitement. A friend of mine that was sitting next to me had an individual sitting in front of him that kept standing up all during the concert. He was really enjoying himself. He would stand up and punch up in the air and jump up and down. Then when he got tired, he would sit down. I don't know for sure, but it's safe to say he was probably drinking. My friend was making comments to me, "This idiot just can't stay in his seat! Or "I should have brought a book to read, seeing how I'm not able to see the concert!" Then at some point during the concert a lot of the people in the row in front of us went somewhere, to get something to eat or use the bathroom, but of course, the guy who was dancing stayed there. He then started using the whole row. He would jump up and down in front of the seats going from side to side with the music. He would dance to the end of the row near the stairs and then change direction and come back to where he was sitting. After about the third time of doing this, he went farther out towards the stairs that you walk up to get to your seat and then out onto the stairs.

Right next to the stairs to get to your seat, was a stairwell to go up or down a level. The stairwells were protected by guardrails to help stop people from going over the edge and falling down the flight to the next level down. This guy was too busy dancing and not paying attention and then proceeded to go right over the guardrail and fall down to the next level onto the cement. It was probably a 10' fall. My friend, who happened to be sitting behind this unfortunate fellow, went down to the end of the row to the railing and looked down the stairs. He came back and said, "Oh yes, that dumb ass split open his melon." "At least I will be able to watch the rest of the concert now!" he said and laughed hysterically. I could not bring myself to go look at the aftermath. But I wanted to. Some different people we had not seen before, came and sat in front of us and one of them started standing up in front of my friend who had the problem earlier. "Oh great," he said. "We get rid of one idiot and there is another to take his place." It seems like that this sort of thing is a part of everyday life.

CHAPTER 6
PERSONS, PLACES, AND THINGS

A lot of the memories we have throughout life are about people, places, and things we may have encountered. This can be on vacation, on the way to work, or simply in an everyday occurrence. It will be something that stands out to you and instills into your memory. Usually, the most awkward occurrence is what you will remember, but it also may be heartfelt or something that really moves you in some way that makes the memory.

I used to think that the people I hung out with were no more important than the dust on glass. But some of the things these individuals did are abnormal compared to most people. For example, a co-worker that I worked with at the local retirement home got to work early as I often did.

We talked for a bit in the parking lot and decided to go drive around before work. I am thinking it was before work anyway because we usually got out of work when it was dark, and it was still light out. Together we were like dynamite. He was the explosive and I was the fuse. I was more of the person who egged people on. I still am to this day. I have always seemed to be able to talk people into doing things. He had an M-80 and we decided while we were driving down a dirt road in my first car, a 1969 Ford Mustang. My friend would light it and throw it out the window. As he lit it and tossed it out the window into the ditch as we kept moving along the road, the dust from the road is stinging our eyes, and we could feel the grit in our mouths. Because the windows were down as far as they go, we were waiting and waiting, driving very slowly.

My friend was looking back out of the window with his head sticking out, and I was watching in the rear-view mirror and it wasn't going off. So, I stop, put it in reverse and start backing up the car. After driving about 10 feet in reverse, BOOM! A momentary blinding flash stuns us. It finally went off when we are almost beside the spot in the ditch where it landed. Both of our ears were ringing as we howled in laughter. Of course, we never thought of any repercussions. We never thought, if it were to have dropped while lit, in the car. Someone could have been hurt, or WORSE.

A different time I was at another friend's home and we were partaking in trying out his parent's alcohol supply, I believe I drank some lime vodka. At the end of the episode we both were quite intoxicated. I remember saying, "Your floors are crooked!" This was because I could not walk straight! We both laughed at our stupidity as we stumbled around his parent's basement for around a couple hours. I didn't know it at the time, but this was the beginning of a long relationship that would last for probably all of my life. Not with the friend, but with partying!

I have always seemed to hang out with people that tend to get in trouble. For instance, the same guy I spoke of earlier that discharged the M-80, used to host small gatherings, maybe 5-8 people, the same circle of friends, every Friday and sometimes Saturday. His parents would go out dancing and be gone till 1:00 or 2:00 in the morning. We would hang out at their house and have some beers. At the time, we were underage, but that did not stop us.

One night my friend and I were sitting on the porch of his parent's home. This home was located in a residential area in the small city of Chelsea, MI. Houses ran up and down the street and the whole street was fully lit up by the street lights. Of course, we had a few drinks. That was the usual thing. Having some drinks among friends, hanging out, and being stupid. This was a well-patrolled area by the local police force. So, one night after we had drank a few beers, we noticed a police car drive by. After it got a little way down the street, my friend, who could do the loudest whistle using the two first fingers in the mouth, lets an ear shattering ringing whistle. He made it sound just like a whistling bottle rocket. The police car comes to a stop. The police car sat stopped in the road for about 15 seconds, but it seemed like a few minutes. Then they started driving again. So, my friend does it again. And the patrol car comes to a complete stop again.

We both were sitting there on pins and needles, trying not to burst out in laughter. It seemed like eternity, but it was just about only 10 seconds. Then suddenly, the police car drove the rest of the way down the street. When the car was out of sight, we howled in laughter at our meek little joke. Yes, we were the kings of the street that night, but it did not go that way every time. Hanging out and having fun can lead to too much fun, and in turn can lead to trouble. And yes, we all got into trouble at one time or another.

A guy I used to hang around in my teens and after high school had a pickup truck that his parents bought him as he was their only child. One night we were out in this person's truck at a lake or something. There happened to be a guardrail that was blocking something that I don't remember. And for some reason, this person decided we needed to bust down this gate. It seemed like a very sturdy guardrail, but this person didn't let that stop him.

While I was sitting in the cab of the truck with the determined driver, this individual rammed the gate about two or three times. After a few minutes, this person got out of the truck and looked at the damage he had done to the gate. "Damn it," he yelled. As he got back in the truck. "I just busted my headlights," he exclaimed." As he jumped back into his truck, looking for me to give him some sort of response like "Good job!" I just sat there laughing, because now he only had one headlight. He left the area in disgust knowing that he had damaged his vehicle and there was no one to blame but himself.

Stories may not always be first hand knowledge. It also may be people that tell you stories or second hand information. My sister Laurel has plenty of her own stories and situations. She used to hang out at Harpo's Bar in Detroit every weekend. She always talked about how people were crazy that attended the establishment. She talked me into going with her and another member of her posse one night.

As we stumbled into the bar, we all realized that we were part of the scene. The band was "Harms Way." They were terrible. It may have had to do with the fact that I was sick with the flu, but I truly believe they were just plain awful. After a few songs, I ventured into the bathroom to release the impending pressure on my bladder. As I walked in, I noticed a poor unfortunate person lying on the floor of the disgusting bathroom. He was not suffering a medical condition that I know of, other than being over medicated with alcohol. I could not, or probably did not want to help.

I noticed that the other people in the bathroom were taking part in trying to revive this unfortunate person and bring him back to consciousness by in urinating on him. I just laughed as I went to the nearest place to relieve myself. I would not want to wake up the next day wondering why I smelled like urine and not remembering passing out in the guy's restroom. Yes, this was a wonderful place. I guess this sort of thing should have been expected after walking into the bar and seeing the condition that the place was in. The seats were torn. There was garbage on the floor. I never went back there again.

A time that is remembered by most of our family, mostly cousins, is when we were all bout 8-10 years old. We talk about the story of "PINK BOY." It was myself and my sister Laurel, my cousin Mike and his sister Rhonda. We were up north in Central Lake, Michigan for relatives wedding. And what sticks out the most from this wedding, besides this memory, is that the wedding cake was a poppy seed cake! Yuck! Anyway, our Grandma Young always had the rule: if we caught the fish and cleaned them, then she would cook them. We caught quite a few blue gills and cleaned them. We were incredibly pleased with the catch and having spent the time involved with all of this, we were looking forward to eating them. We had left the cleaned fish in a bucket of water outside the basement door while we went in to talk to Grandma.

When we came back outside, we were dumbfounded to see the bucket was now gone! We went upstairs into the house and ask my grandmother if she had taken the bucket of fish? "Nope," she replied. After looking around for a while, someone spotted the bucket out on the dock way down from the house down at the lake. When we went down there, the fish (that were now dead) were in the water, lying on the bottom of the lake floor, which was about 3 or 4 feet at the dock. We were wondering what had happened, when a boy about our age walked down to the dock where we were at and proudly pronounced, "I threw them in the water." I guess it did not matter to him that they were dead and cleaned, and would not be swimming away, but he did it anyway. I do not remember much about this time, except that this punk, whom we had observed many times throughout the day, was wearing a pink polo like shirt. So, we dubbed him PINK BOY!

He was on my grandmother and Grandfather's turf, so we vowed vengeance. Not that we would ever see this person again in our lives, as we did not even know who he was, or why he was on the premises. We were all deeply disappointed from this. What could we do? We left my Grandparents that weekend feeling defeated to say the least. The moment was forgotten by all of us kids. A few months later, the gang of us was again up North, as we seemed to do when we were younger. This time we were in Suttons Bay, MI. at my Great Aunt and uncles house, visiting and relaxing for the weekend. The property included a cherry orchard that I worked on one summer.

My cousin Mike and I were just lounging around the property when one of our sisters came up to us older guys and said, "Hey, remember Pink Boy?" One of us said, "Of course, how could we forget?" They excitedly replied, "Well he is HERE."

My cousin and I looked at each other and said at the same time, "Show us." I don't remember if he had on his pink shirt, or how they even recognized this kid, but all of the Young and Smith kids marched to where this kid was, I guess playing, or whatever he was doing. He was up on top of a small dirt quarry located on my Uncle Jerry's property. It probably seemed like a mountain to him and us, since we were all kids. We all stood around him, like vultures getting ready to devour their prey.

Either my cousin or my self, or both of us, said, "Hey do you remember that time you were at a house and you dumped someone's fish that they had caught back in the lake"? He had to have said "Yes," because we yelled back at him, "WELL THAT WAS US"! And this part of the story is a little blurry as to who did the deed. But either my older Cousin or myself proceeded to push the kid off the edge of the hill and he rolled down the hill like a used tire, rolling and finally hitting the bottom. He ran crying to whomever he was with, and we all just stood there atop this dirt quarry, proud of what we had just done. According to others who were there, we all got scolded for being "bullies" against this poor helpless child, but we knew we had just settled the score in the war of "family vs. pink boy." To this day the cousins still talk about this. And none of us know to this day, who this person was, or why he was at our family gatherings. I wonder if this person ever thinks about being pushed down a dirt hill by "bullies" as a kid. I know we will not forget him.

If we experience something, whether it pertains to a person, a certain place or any other situation, we most likely will remember it if it is entertaining enough or if it is endearing to the heart. I started taking a lot of pictures when I am out on vacation to capture the moment and to help me remember in more detail. I like to be able to tell a story with accuracy.

I decided later in life, that I wanted to see certain things in the United States before I died, or even if they were no longer there. I used to tell people, "I want to see it before it's blown up or taken down or you are not allowed to see something like we have been able to in the past. Like for instance, you can't go inside the Hoover Dam anymore. My wife probably thought I was being overly dramatic saying a monument may be blown up at some point and would just laugh it off. But at this writing, statues are being torn down, things are being taken away, so I guess I had some sort of clairvoyance. So, I like to utilize the American dream, and vacation. I like to see different things. Hear the things in the environment and smell the smells.

For instance, seeing the Statue of Liberty, not to only see the statue but to feel the stones it is built out of. To see the crumbling walls of the Alcatraz prison and taste the burning saltwater on your breath. To sit in the seat of the "Spruce Goose", (Howard Hughes's) magnificent masterpiece of a plane and to feel the brittle leather prickling at your skin as you sit in the cockpit. To be in Dealey Plaza in Dallas Texas and feel the strange eerie feeling run up and down your spine, to know that you are in an area that a US President was assassinated. Yes, these are all places I have been, and encourage all Americans to visit. It's stimulating to the senses to see new places. To experience the visual and perhaps other senses you may encounter when visiting historic sites. I think most of my memories are from visual senses, as are most people.

Some memories may be inspired and recalled by that which you have smelled. We have walked into places like the Cheers bar, in Boston Massachusetts, that was certainly a nasal sense, because of the fish smell. We walked into the establishment, but my wife immediately smelled the sea food smell, the searing fish smell that seemed to engulf the senses and seemed to set itself in our nasal cavities like we were there catching the fish on the boat. My wife said, "I can't take this, it will make me sick," so needless to say we didn't eat at the world famous Cheers bar, we just have pictures of the outside.

Seeing sites and monuments throughout the US gives you memories that are engrained in your memory, by sight, sound, and smell. I tend to think it's mostly sight, but in certain places it may be other senses. Like The Muir forest in California, you smell the trees and hear the wildlife. You can hear the birds singing their songs and it makes you appreciate the peaceful, tranquility of the parks, versus the loud noises and business of the cities. You can spend a day, reuniting yourself with the wilderness. And Muir woods is also the site for filming of Return of The Jedi.

Spending time in Washington DC, even though when you think about Washington DC, all you think about is corrupt politicians, wasteful spending of taxpayer dollars, and just a complete waste of time, is actually something everyone should see. Because it all is free! The Lincoln Memorial, the World War 2 Memorial, the Washington Monument, the Vietnam Memorial, the Jefferson Memorial, the FDR Memorial, the

MLK Memorial and the White House. Just the craftsmanship alone that went into all of these places, so long ago is quite mesmerizing.

Something I learned in Washington that I never knew or had heard before, was the information about the Washington Monument. The monument was started in 1848, using private funding from donations and construction continued until the money dried up in 1856, at which time the construction halted and the monument stood unfinished at a height of 156'. The monument remained in this state for 20 years, until in 1776, Congress appropriated funds to complete the construction, but it was another 3 years before construction actually resumed, because they were in arguments about how the rest of the monument was to be designed.

So even back then, it took the government years to get anything done! So, construction resumed in 1879, and in 1885 the monument is dedicated. But the main highlight that we heard about the monument on all the bus tours, was that if you look at the monument, it is two different colors. A darker tan stone near the bottom and white stone the rest of the way up. That's because when construction halted, 20 years past between then and when it re-started, and the new stone came from different quarries. And once completed, the Washington Monument was the tallest building in the world at 555'. There is also a stipulation for buildings in Washington. They can only be of a certain maximum height. It is so that the Washington Monument can easily be seen.

Now on the other hand, sometimes it is cool to be among the hustle-bustle of the big city and hear the constant honking of the cars like in Manhattan, sitting in gridlock in Times Square. When we were visiting New York, we witnessed an ambulance coming through the middle of Times Square, trying to find any little opening between the cars to get them closer to who ever was in need. They made it through somehow, but there is something about New York. The constant honking as the lights turns green, to hear the "click clack" of the marching people making their daily trek to wherever they may be off to.

Smelling the smoky exhaust of the passing trucks and cars as they hiss by you like a racecar. The hustle and bustle are also businesses operating and people making purchases. The fishy smell that fills the wharf of San Francisco bay is all part of this. Walking the boardwalk along the wharf the seafood smell soon becomes part of you. You can almost taste the salt from the ocean lining the inside of your mouth. And of course, after walking all day near the docks, once you get back to your room, you smell like the fish that are caught everyday at the docks. So have pleasant dreams!

So, I think it's cool to look back, and be able to think back, about certain cool things I have seen or places I have been, or things I have done. I tend to do this by watching video slide shows I have made of my vacations. It helps you to relive the moments and take you back to things you saw and experienced that you may had forgot.

While in Hawaii, my cousin Sarah and I went in a shark cage with sharks in the water. They were about eight-foot long! I can't remember the types of sharks, but there were no great whites! I have been on the memorial, above the USS Arizona. It was very sobering to be there where this battle happened. It's hard to imagine that such a pretty and quiet place was once a place of great tragedy and loss of American lives. A funny story, my cousin Sarah decided she wanted to feed the pigeons, by placing a Dorito in her mouth and letting them take it. We laughed ourselves silly when it finally happened. I snorkeled at a coral reef and had an eel swim right underneath me. I just remained motionless as the fear gripped me and I just sort of floated in place as the eel just simply swam by. I climbed up an extinct volcano, which is called Diamond Head. I saw an authentic Luau and simply enjoyed paradise on earth. I didn't want to leave. I think I could live there!

In New York City or Manhattan, I saw the Statue of Liberty and walked on the base at her feet. I would have walked up to the crown, but tickets had been sold out. I went all the way to the top of the Empire State Building to the 102nd floor.

Personally, I thought the 86th floor observatory deck had better views. On the 102nd floor it's enclosed with Plexiglas. I walked in Central Park and just outside of Central Park, I saw the spot where John Lennon was shot and killed. I saw the tomb and resting-place of President General Grant. I toured the aircraft carrier Intrepid. I stood out in front of the restaurant called Sparks Steakhouse, where John Gotti and other associates murdered a mobster boss named Paul Castillano in 1985. I visited another establishment that used to be a barbershop where another mobster named Albert Anastasia was murdered in 1957. There was a restaurant in little Italy where yet again another mobster named Joe Gallo was gunned down in the early 1970's. I wanted to visit this as well, but we ran out of time.

In Tampa, Florida I held a 3-foot alligator and I road on an airboat, feeling the air rip my hair as the boat zips in and around the channels.

When I visited Universal Studios in Florida, there are a couple things that I remember specifically. First the Jurassic Park area of the park. You could have your picture taken with a Raptor. You stood next to an 8'-10' cement wall enclosing the creature. All you could see behind the wall were woods and jungle. When you were against the wall, the workers would say, "Ok, when the Raptor shows up, just remain as still as possible. DO NOT make any sudden movements. I did not know what to expect. They called it by name, let us say "Tommy." The worker called out "Come on Tommy, come see the people who are here for you." Then you heard rustling in the forest, behind the wall.

As it got closer, you also started to hear some growling and then roars. Then suddenly, the head of a Raptor was sitting there right by my head. I was too scared to move. So, I looked out of the corner of my eye and it was looking back and forth at my wife Anna and I. It would sniff me, and you could feel the warm breath from its mouth full of razor-sharp teeth as it breathed on you. Then it moved toward my wife and it was breathing heavy on her through its nostrils, blowing her hair around as it did this. I was on the verge of believing that Universal Studios had captured a real live Raptor and were allowing the public to see it. It was THAT REAL.

The second thing I remember specifically from Universal Studios was the horror show. We watched a special effects man, who has worked in many movies, show his handy work. He showed us his blood pops that go off when the gun that is pointed at them triggers them to go off. And it looks life like.

He was walking around the stage with a machete stuck in his forehead, and it looked so real. I wanted to ask him if he needed an ambulance! It's so great to have these special effects to make an otherwise boring life, feel over the top alive, even if it's for only a few moments. Also, in Universal Studios Florida Orlando, they had a plastic shark hanging up, from the old Jaws ride. The movie was from 1975, and the attraction opened in 1976, but was closed in 2012. So, me being the clown, stuck my head in the mouth of the plastic shark, hanging upside down from its tail, and stood there for the photo with my arms extended out. It is funnier if you see the picture.

In Dallas, Texas, I have stood up on the exact spot that Abraham Zapruter filmed the Kennedy assassination in Dealey Plaza. It is hard to imagine that such a quiet spot when we were there happened to be the same spot that a US President was assassinated. I was just silent while standing there, visualizing the horror that played out in 1963 as the motorcade drove through the area. That was probably the main reason for me wanting to go there. Sorry if it's a bit macob.

In New Mexico, I saw Billy the Kid's grave, in Fort Sumter, New Mexico. I stood in the courthouse that Billy the Kid escaped from and killed a Sheriff and Deputy. Also, in New Mexico is the city of Roswell. I drove by the general area where a spacecraft was supposed to have crashed in 1947. There is nothing to see there, other than desert. So, if you want to feel the sun beating down on you, and feel the grit in your teeth from the wind blowing the dust at you, check out Roswell New Mexico and go look for aliens!

While in Boston, Massachusetts, I stood at the helm of the USS Constitution, the oldest surviving US warship. Also, while we were in Boston, I stood at the spot that the British murdered residents in the Boston Massacre. I also stood at the end of the finish line of the Boston marathon where the terrorist's bomb went off wounding and killing many people in 2013. I walked up to the top of the 221' tall Bunker Hill Monument. And was in the exact area where the Boston Tea Party happened. We even got to throw mock boxes of tea over the side of the boat.

In San Francisco California, I stood at the jail cell doors that held Frank Morris, John, and Clarence Anglin before they escaped from Alcatraz Prison in June 1962. Spending time in the prison and out on the prison grounds was a fun experience. I got to walk around the recreation yard where many hardened criminals once walked. I was amazed at the walls that enclosed the yard. I bet they were 12-15 feet tall and had barbed wire on top. I rode across the Golden Gate Bridge in San Francisco, California. And also visited Yosemite National Park.

While spending time in Oregon, I sat in the same cockpit seat that Howard Hughes sat in his plane, the Spruce Goose which is now located in McMinnville, Oregon. To know that you are sitting where Howard Hughes once sat is cool. This was the main reason for me going to Oregon. There are very wonderful sites that include waterfalls and hiking trails, but we were unable to do this because a teenager from Washington decided to set off fireworks during a heat wave and he proceeded to burn over 48,000 acres of wooded area. He was ordered to pay 37 Million in restitution. Man, I would hate to have that in my conscience all my life!

Visiting Washington DC, I toured the White House, and while you only got to see the East Wing, which is where meetings happen, and special events, it's still neat to say you have been there. One night while we were walking back from a day of sightseeing, suddenly, a swarm of police showed up, and closed down the street. As I was stuck behind some barriers, I watched a parade of black SUV's come up the street and turn into the road that leads to the White House. I had heard earlier that a British Diplomat was scheduled to be at the White House for a meeting, so we got to see that. YES, that is the only thing I saw of this caliber. Now I was impressed by the police and secret service presence, which I guess you would expect in Washington DC, and how polite and friendly they were.

I spent a good part of the day in Arlington Cemetery, which if you visit Washington DC, you should go to Arlington Cemetery in Virginia, which is across the river. Arlington Cemetery is upwards of 600 acres, which is extraordinary. To think that most of the people in the cemetery fought for you and I to have the rights that we do is something you have to remember. I visited most of the Smithsonian museums while in Washington

DC, and one of them was the American History Museum. It was one of the best museums to visit, and one of the things that sticks out was we saw Dorothy's ruby slippers and Glinda the good Witch's Wand from the movie The Wizard of Oz. There were many, many things to see in Washington DC.

While visiting Tombstone, Arizona. I stood near the OK Corral where the famous shootout happened between the Earp's, the Clanton's, and McCleary's. I stood in the Boot Hill Cemetery where people killed at the OK Corral are buried, where it states on the cowboy's tombstone "Murdered in the streets of Tombstone 1881." I was only there about four hours and I think you need to spend a day there. I would like to go back. I saw the Red Rock Mountains of Arizona, which was the location of the Church of the Red Rocks, which was a church, built into the side of the Red Rock Mountain. I also visited the huge crater made by a meteor millions of years ago. There were 100 MPH winds that day. I was amazed at how hard it was to maneuver up and down the stairs to see the full view of the site because of the wind. It was a struggle. You wanted to make sure you had the handrail for the stairs on the opposite side of the wind to help steady you. I had never experienced that before.

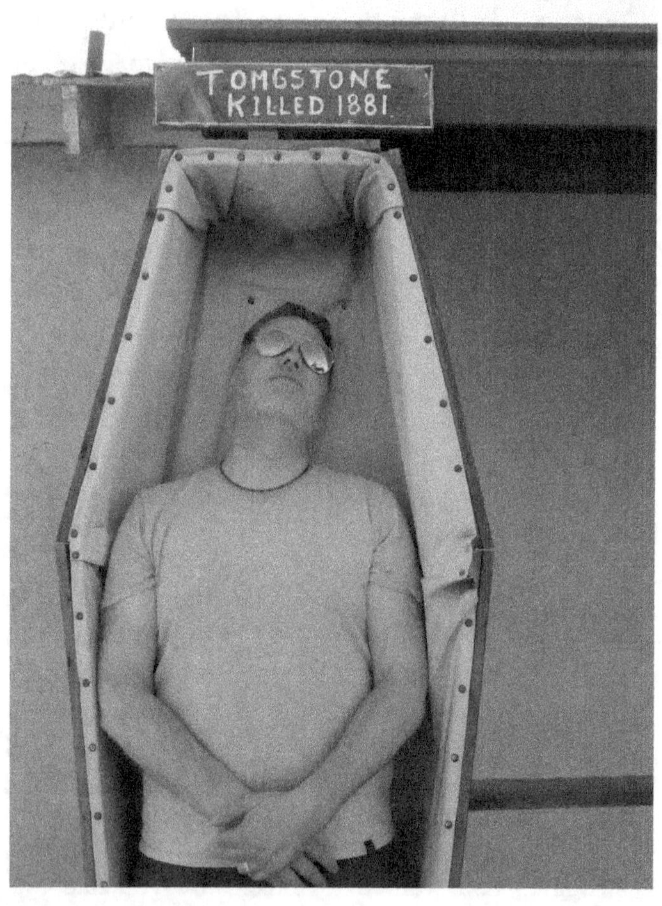

To see the Las Vegas Strip is also a must do thing in life. It is literally another world in the United States. All the glowing neon that seems to cover you in a glaze of wonderful light and make you part of the city that never sleeps. Even spending a week there, you seem rushed. One of the things I did was rent a Corvette for a day. It was great. I have always wanted one and even having one for a day is a wonderful experience.

Driving around Nevada with the top down feeling the wind blow through your hair and feeling the warm presence of the sun was very relaxing and added to the experience. It only makes me want a Corvette more! The other highlight for me was shooting some machine guns. Machine guns are legal in Las Vegas. At least at the shooting range. Shooting a "Tommy Gun" was awesome. Yes, a 1928 50 round drum .45 caliber Thompson machine gun. Also shooting the Browning automatic Rifle, or the BAR for short, was really cool. The BAR was also the preferred weapon of Clyde Barrow of the infamous "Bonnie and Clyde." I also shot an MG 42, which was the preferred weapon of the Germans in World War Two. I was amazed at how quick the gun shot through 50 rounds. I certainly have admiration for our young soldiers that stormed the beaches at Normandy while facing this wicked weapon firing upon them. Going to Las Vegas once is defiantly not enough. No sooner were we back home, I was ready to go back to see things we did not see the first time. There is always a new vacation planned with us! We tend to have a new vacation planned about 1 year in advance!

When on vacation I always seem to grab some bread from breakfast at the hotel to feed the ducks. It is just something I like that is relaxing. You can start with just a couple around you, but it doesn't take long for more and more to show up to have their chance to be fed too. By the end, I feel like

Dr. Doolittle with a swarm of ducks around me. When sitting outside at a restaurant, there usually is a small bird or two looking for scraps and of course, I must give them something too. Whenever I see the little birds looking for any scraps that have fallen to the ground. I am always compelled to throw a French fry or two on the ground for them. They always seem thankful! And if they could speak English, I am sure they would say, "Thank you sir, may I have another?" as they sit there looking up at you waiting for the next morsel of food you may possibly throw to them.

I feel blessed that I have been able to experience all of these places within about a ten-year period. All of these places and things are reasons why we take pictures, so when we get to the point that we don't remember anymore, you still have that memory. Sometimes you are not lucky enough to get a picture, so you only have a memory. Thus, the reason to write it down before you forget it. That is one of the reasons why I'm writing things down. I don't have pictures of everything, so I better write it down before it's forgotten.

Chapter 7
Employment And Memories

During someone's lifetime they may get a job and they are employed with that company until they retire. Other people have many employers throughout their lifetime. I fall into the latter category. A total of 13 companies I have worked for. One of them twice, as you will read about later. The reason, for me anyway is not because I just can't hold a job, but more of a variety of reasons. A quest to make more money, I didn't like the work I was doing, job was too repetitive, the employer was mis-managed, or even termination!

My first job ever was mowing the cemetery at my church I attended. So, I guess I have had 14 jobs! I remember I made 50.00 every time I mowed the lawn and trimmed around the gravestones.

That kind of money was not too bad for a kid about 10 or twelve years old around 1982. Sometimes the temperature would be in the 90's and I would have to take many breaks resting in the church basement because I would get a terrible headache from the heat while I was hand mowing the cemetery. Sometimes my Mom and Dad would help do the trimming. I think this was a good first job to give the individual a taste of manual labor.

My first "real" job was at the local A&W restaurant. This place was run by a couple of probably retired people just looking for something to do with the money they had and a way to occupy some time. It was family run, so both of their daughters worked there as managers. I soon found out this place was what we in the employment industry call a "dump." They paid very little, yelled at you when you made a mistake and were just not good employers. I made a bad mistake early in my "career."

I was cleaning up for the night. I was busy mopping and the manager Mary said, "Don't mop the girls bathroom yet, I have to use the bathroom, so give it a minute." I must have not really been listening, even though I probably said, "ok." A few minutes later, I walked into the girl's bathroom, totally forgetting what I was just told, to see Mary, probably straight in front of me, sitting on the toilet with her dress to her feet. "What the hell" she screamed, "get out," she yelled with deafening power. I had embarrassed her obviously and needless to say, even though it was an accident, she always had it out for me after that. I was paid 3.35, which was minimum wage at the time. So, there was not much motivation to work too hard.

The other daughter was pretty nice and I liked her. She knew the employee moral was low and how things were there. She said one night half seriously "You guys better get moving on what you need to do or I will have to fire you." Myself and the other employee both pretty much said very sarcastically, "Oh no, please! Not that." It was the truth. I finally got fed up with everything and just didn't go in one day. Boy were they mad about that. I didn't care. It was retribution.

My next employment was at the local Retirement home in Chelsea, Michigan. I have many fond memories of this place. I rose in financial status to 5.50 an hour. I soon became a star worker. Working in many different positions in the dietary department. I had a lot of fun working there, creating many different situations that were both embraced and frowned upon. I decided to play a joke on the supervisor on duty. I poured red food coloring all over my hand, walked up to her, as I looked to be in great distress, and while presenting my red food colored hand in front of me, said, "I think I need to go to the hospital." She said, "OH MY GOD!" but I said, "Just kidding, it's just food coloring." She was not pleased.

I would work from 4 p.m. to 8 p.m. at the retirement home because I was still in high school. We would serve the food, then clean the kitchen before going home. I locked up the kitchen and was the last one out of the department many times. I would take food home with me any chance I got. I would take juice, chocolate milk, yogurt, ice cream, pudding or leftovers from dinner. I even took a whole pie one time.

Yes, I know, I was not a good, honest employee. On one occasion, the same person who lit the M-80 and myself had to deliver trays of food to a couple of the resident's rooms. This would happen from time to time when a person was a little under the weather or maybe even too sick to go down to the main dining hall with all of the residents for dinner. So, we would personally deliver the tray of food to the residents room. While on the way to deliver the trays of food, there was a sitting area by some elevators. It would be mainly be used by residents who may get fatigued while on the way to the dining room and back to their room from dinner. The co-worker walked into the area, sat down in one of the chairs, which happened to have a small table in front of it and sat the tray he was carrying down on the table.

He uncovered the food and started to eat a couple of the chicken nuggets, which happened to be the main course of the meal. I was flabbergasted. I asked him, "What in the heck are you doing?" He replied back ever so calmly as if he wasn't doing anything wrong, while still chewing and said, "I'm hungry." I didn't agree with this at all. I shook my head in utter disappointment and said to him as I continued on to deliver my tray, "That's low." I don't think I had much respect for this individual after that.

Working at the retirement home, my job required me at times, to deliver meals to residents who were too sick to make it down to the dining room. On one occasion, I knocked on the door to the resident's room. "Come in," I heard a female voice reply. I walked in and found an elderly woman sitting on the floor of her living room with a large gash on the bridge of her nose. There was blood all over her face and all over the front of her shirt where it had flowed out of the wound downward all over the front of her. I asked her if she was ok and she said, "Oh yes, I just fell and didn't want to bother the nurse." I said, "It is no bother, if something like this happens, please call for a nurse!" I stayed with the poor woman until the nurse arrived to tend to her.

On another occasion, I was delivering a meal to a resident who was too sick to make it to the dining room. I knocked on the door to the room. I got no answer. I knocked louder and still got no answer. Against my better judgement, I slowly turned the doorknob to the room and it was not locked. I proceeded to open the door and it opened. "Hello?" I said as I slowly opened the door trying not to intrude, yet still opening the door and slowly walking in the room to investigate.

As I walked in the door, I noticed an elderly woman lying on the floor of the room between the bedroom and the bathroom. The light was on in the bathroom. I said, "Ma'am, are you ok?" I got no response from the woman. I ran back out of the room out into the hallway to the nearest phone and called into the intercom. "Nurse to room (whatever the room number was) STAT." The word STAT in health terms means immediately. I stood outside the door of the room only a matter of a minute or two, before two nurses from the main unit arrived. I pointed them to the room and they hurried in. They checked for some vital signs, but found the woman on the floor to be unresponsive. So, this was the first time I found a dead body. When I got back to the kitchen, my female co-worker exclaimed "Gee, take your time, we don't need your help!" I told her, "Hey, I just found a dead body." "No way?" she screamed back at me, as this was the first time this had happened. It was a memorable moment for me in time.

While still working at the retirement home, I decided one day that I was hungry, so I went into the cooler and grabbed a yogurt. I opened in and poured it into my mouth, sort of drinking it. I came out of the cooler and threw the empty container into the trash and took my place on the food line to put together food trays for the residents. The supervisor looked at me and said, "Did you just eat something"? "No," I said with a tone in my voice that I was flabbergasted to be even asked the question. The female supervisor asked again

"Don't lie to me, did you just eat something"? "No," I replied with more emphasis in my voice, thinking that would take care of the situation. She then said very lovingly, "Well I know you are lying, because you have yogurt on your nose!"

I was embarrassed to be caught in this lie. I said sorry and that was the end of it. The only time I really got in trouble there was when we had a butter fight. What is a butter fight you ask? You take the little sealed butter packs, point them at your victim and squeeze on the end facing you. The same supervisor that caught me in my yogurt lie pulled me in the office and wrote me up. Apparently wasting packs of butter was the last straw!

I finally put in my notice of termination when I got turned down for a position that I could have handled with ease. It was a true case of discrimination, I felt because the manger was a lesbian and she gave to position to a female that was SSLLOOWWW at the job and was not really capable. So, I gave my exit papers!

I then preceded to a company called Colorbok that made note pads. I remember in the interview, the manager asked me what kind of a car I had. I thought it was odd. You would ask if someone had a car, but not necessarily the make of the vehicle. "I drive a Trans Am," I replied very proudly to him. Cool he said and hired me on the spot. I found out later the manager was a lover of muscle cars and had one himself, so my car may have helped. This was another place where I made a lot of friends and had a lot of fun.

Right next door to our building was a building where one of the people I worked with rented space to work on cars as a side business. Another guy rented the rest of the building to do wood working. I became friends with the mechanic and spent a lot of time after work having beers in the woodshop. I started to notice as we hung out after work in the wood shop building, a lot of people coming in and out of the place spending a short time in the office and then leaving. I didn't think much of it. I thought it must be clients. We continued our partying.

We named one of the guys that partied with us "Jethro", because he got mad at his car, kicked it for whatever reason and broke his foot. A couple times, a guy showed up with his Great Dane. This dog was massive. And the dog was very friendly. We enjoyed having him around. One night this gentleman showed up without "Jocko," as the dog was called. A coworker named Curtis and myself asked, "Where is Jocko?" The man replied, "He is back at home". We probably yelled back "We have to go get him; he needs to be here."

We proceeded to talk the dog owner into driving about 15 or 20 minutes to his house with both Curtis and myself tin the truck to get the animal. The man seemed to have no problem driving to get his dog. We got to his home, loaded up the dog in the bed of the truck, so of course Curtis and myself rode in the bed with Jocko during the ride back to the woodshop. We had been drinking of course and were standing up in the bed and were leaning over the cab. The wind whipped through our hair as we went along. I can't imagine what would have happened if a police officer would have seen us.

We enjoyed the rest of our time that night along with our K9 friend! Sometime later, the police raided the wood shop next door to Colorbok. The wood worker had been dealing marijuana out of the shop. He went to prison for a few years. I actually saw him years later in one of my college classes after he was out of prison.

A couple of stories I remember during my tenure at Colorbok, I became a good friend with one of the truck drivers that delivered supplies to us. He even came to one of our Christmas parties! One day he showed up in his full-length semi truck and came up to us as he always did to get it uploaded. I asked him one of those questions that I was sure the answer was going to be no. I asked "Hey, can I drive your truck across the parking lot"? I was totally surprised when he said "Have at it, keys are in it"! I got up into the Semi, started it and drove it from one end of the parking lot to the other. Pretty cool!

Another memory I have is that some people were out in the parking lot during brake time and were throwing a football back and forth. I wouldn't have been doing that, because of all of the cars there. My co-worker Todd made the comment, "If that football touches my car, there will be blood spilled in the parking lot!" Never a dull moment at Colorbok! I got tired of being employed by Colorbok for some reason, which escapes me, but I didn't want to quit. I wanted to be fired so I could collect unemployment for a while, so I went into work drunk one day.

Before work, I hung out at an old party house I will discuss later, with a friend and drank mixed vodka drinks mostly. Probably some beers too! I remember the day perfectly. I was working afternoons at the time (which may have added to my wanting to be fired!) I arrived at the job quite blitzed. After about an hour I was called into the manager's office. They said they were terminating me because they felt I was not contributing my best. There was no mention of the fact that I was obliterated at the time!

While I sat there in the office with the manager and the HR person, I said, "You know", as I sat up in my seat and cleared my throat, so they could hear my statement clearly. "This is the best thing that could ever happen to me!" I felt this was a great declaration! Later, I found out from a co-worker I kept in touch with, that the HR person had said, "I can't believe he said that." I got my unemployment, which was all I cared about.

I went to community college for cad and drafting and I got a job at a company called Michigan Trenching that installed gas lines for such companies like Consumers Energy and DTE. I completed the drafting for the final installs. This was what I had gone to school for! This was the job of a lifetime! I worked for this company through the years, until it became Exelon and then was bought by Infrasource. I thought this might be the company I retire from. But in 2008, the economy took a dive and businesses such as the one I worked for felt the repercussions of the economy.

There was an Ohio project that happened at a time when we were all very low on work. A bunch us of took the project to be able to stay working. The Ohio project called "Wilderness" kept us all busy working for the next year or so. Because of that we were thankful! Myself, my friend Pete, my friend Lloyd and our boss and friend Jim were a small number of people involved with the project.

One story I remember, is working out of town in Ohio for one of these companies and that we were allowed to buy groceries for the week. You would turn in the expenses at the end of the week, and get reimbursed by the company. Three other co-workers and myself sort of made it a game to see who would up with the largest grocery bill. I can proudly say I held the record for the grocery bill at 194.00 for a week.

At that time, I was planning on getting laid off at the end of the job, so I was buying extras, to have to live on when that happened. I had taken a picture of my pantry, and it was jam packed with everything, plus there was stuff stored in the basement. I wish I still had that picture. I was so proud. My co-workers were also, I think! I even tried to get reimbursed for toothpaste and a new belt on one of the occasions.

At the end of the project, I was laid off after 11 years with the company. It was devastating. You can't understand it unless it really happens to you. At least I prepared for the lay off and had a ton of food that was bought by expensing the Ohio project. So, after I was laid off, I still lived pretty well because of planning!

CHAPTER 8
DANGEROUS TIMES

Some people live their lives by the seat of their pants. Some people say we as individuals control our own destiny, from childhood to adulthood. There are those who believe we all are in control of our lives, no matter what the situation we are in. Others say if you grow up in a crime-ridden area, you will be a criminal. Others say if you are brought up in the best of surroundings, you will be the best citizen. I do not know about all of that, but what I think is that an individual probably has some control over their destiny. So, if they want to be a criminal, they will. You have to take into account many factors and variables. I truly believe no one can really say for certain.

I find it fascinating to find out about all the people in our family that have served in the military. Among those are: my Aunt Connie, my father, my cousin Mike and farther back in time, my Grandpa Hughes who fought in World War two and ended up being a POW. There was also my great Grandfather Newman Young who fought in World War one and my great, great, great Grandfather Theodore Chapin who fought in the civil war. Thank you all for serving your country and protecting our freedom. I have recently found information that while fighting in the civil war on January 1863, Mr. Theodore Chapin was wounded in the heel during battle. The wound was diagnosed in the war hospital as Erysipelas, a rapidly spreading inflammation of the skin known in the middle ages as "St Anthony's fire". The germs get into the breaks of the skin and spread quickly. He lingered in the hospital as the disease ate flesh off his leg. It eventually spread throughout his body until he died from his wounds in June of 1863. What a painful way to have to die!

I suppose the better question is not what you have done in your life, but have you ever saved another human being? I have been told that I have, though I don't remember doing it. My sister Laurel told me that she remembered that in our younger years, I had possibly saved her life! She remembered that when we were kids, she had eaten something that made her start choking. She could not breathe. The piece of food was stuck in her throat.

My sister Laurel told me that I acted as though I had been waiting for this moment with the tools I had been taught at some point in time. I immediately performed the Heimlich maneuver on Laurel as she was choking on a piece of food. I grabbed her from behind and placed my arms around her stomach area and proceeded to pull my arms in on her stomach as I had learned in school. As I did this, after a few pushes, the piece of food that was causing the problem came out of her mouth. I don't remember doing this, but Laurel assures me that this happened.

If you strive for something more than what you are given in life and work hard for it, then you may have a chance to get it. I didn't take on this philosophy until much later in life, unfortunately. As I stated earlier, I have not led the greatest or most wholesome life. I may have done bad things in life. When I was younger, myself and a couple of neighborhood hoodlums liked to roam around the block, inflicting our version of justice to the unfortunate peoples home's in our path, that we deemed fit. We would "TP" or toilet paper the trees of houses. We would ring doorbells and run off for the owner of the home to come to the door to see no one. One time I was out with two or three neighborhood kids and we decided that we should do the doorbell trick on my uncle Jeff that lived nearby to my parents. I rang the doorbell and then sprinted around to the end of the house and hide around the corner. Believing I was so cunning and smart, I stood there watching the door that we just rang the doorbell at, patiently waiting for my uncle to fall for the prank. After a few seconds, which always seem like minutes, I happened to look up at the dark window that was above me, that I was standing under and my uncle was standing there looking out the window at us. I as well as the people that were with me walked to the front door, scorned as we were caught. My uncle opened his front door and said, "That's a good way to get shot." I said "Sorry." We left that night with our tails between our legs, but we learned from that lesson. One night a few of us local neighborhood kids decided to get together to go do "whatever." We stopped off at a local neighborhood boy that we hung out with to try to see if we could get him to come out. We tapped on his bedroom window, while whispering his name. After about a minute of doing this, his father ripped open the drapes to his room standing there looking at us, and we all took off running away. I never heard anything about this as far as repercussions for trying to get the neighborhood kid out of bed.

All of this sounds tame right? Well, it elevated from there, I think. I started to hang around with a different group of neighborhood kids and we started to terrorize the neighborhood. We went to a home that had a broken-down car or two in the yard. We showed our dislike of this by breaking the windows of the vehicles in the yard. Shooting the windows out with sling shots, or whatever we found along the way to break windows.

There were a couple of teachers that lived in the area of all of us hoodlums, so they were in our web of destruction. One teacher in particular, we always HEAVILY toilet papered his home. I don't know how he got it out of his tall trees, as we threw it up very high. And living next door to him was a more hated teacher. We treated him as such. He used to particular tell his students, "If you toilet paper me, you are just making it hard for my wife, because she is the one who cleans it up!" We did not let that stop us. We probably used (3) 12 paper rolls on his house one night. Yes, that is 36 rolls. As we were there, I noticed a volleyball net they had set up in the yard for their children to play with. I happened to have a knife with me for some reason and I proceeded to cut the volleyball net right down the center. Then I noticed at the same house, a tire swing. An innocent tire swing for a child to play on, that probably brought hours of joy to the children of the household. I walked right over to it, pulled out my knife and with glee, cut it down. I watched the tire bounce a few times before it hit the ground and wobbled a bit up and down before coming to a final rest.

We also smashed metal mailboxes of various people we found we didn't care for, or looked down upon. To be honest, I don't remember what we would smash it with. I'm sure we didn't carry a baseball bat around with us. I think we just grabbed a large branch that would be lying on the ground. One mailbox in particular, which belonged to a family that lived near the end of the road we lived on, was constantly smashed up. We finally got tired of looking at the smashed-up excuse for a mailbox still sitting atop it's post, overlooking the fact that it was because of us, the group of local hoodlums, that made it that way.

We tore the box off the post threw it to the ground and stomped on it which caused the rivets in the sides to explode out and the thing just fell apart. We left it laying in pieces on the ground next to the road. The next day riding the bus, I happened to be sitting on the side that this now destroyed mailbox was on. And what was icing on the cake was that the children of this large family lined up for the bus right next to the mailbox. They were pointing and looking at it right up to the time they entered the bus. For some strange reason I found this wonderfully satisfying. I guess I'm lucky I never wound up in Juvenile hall, or worse yet, Prison!

So, as you have noticed our family rode the bus to school when we were younger. We seemed to have a few different bus drivers over about a ten-year period. Most of them were very nice. I even remember at least one of them, at the end of the school year, would take the whole busload on the last day of the school year to the local Dairy Queen in Chelsea, for an ice cream cone. One year she even paid for "dipped" cones if we wanted them. That driver was the best! But there is one bus driver that REALLY stands out in my memory. And it isn't because she was nice. She was the last one I had until I was able to drive and not have to ride the confounded bus anymore to school.

We had a bus driver one year that was not very nice. No one seemed to like her. This driver, right from the start tried to show us who was the boss (her). She would kick people off the bus and that was the ultimate punishment if you were a kid riding the bus. She kicked a fellow so-called hoodlum friend I associated with, off the bus for "Threatening to shoot another bus patron with a .22 GAGUE" Yes, this is exactly what the "kick off" slip read. The bus driver did not even spell it right. The father of my buddy that got kicked off the bus because of what the bus driver claimed said to us, "I'm not signing this slip because I agree with her stupidity, I'm signing it because I want my kid to be able to get to the damn school."

We felt this was an insult to us, so we decided to make the bus divers life drivers life a living hell while having to drive us to school! We did up a mural for the driver and placed it in a strategic area along the route. And did I mention the bus driver was a heavyset woman? So, we drew a picture of an elephant driving a bus while looking in the mirror to watch the people on the bus. It was a great picture, so we thought. I am not sure if she even saw it. Oh, the terrible and stupid things we do as kids! One week a person who got kicked off the bus previously walked on at his stop with a novelty elephant trunk hanging of his nose. We all laughed, but the bus driver seemed to be less then amused, but our greatest feat against her was still to come.

On one occasion, during the bus ride, it was a normal day. As we went down a dirt road to drop off school children that lived down the road. We were fuming about the driver for whatever reason during this day. We always seemed to be at odds against the bus driver because of her pushback to try to show her superiority over us. One of the times during a drop off, we certainly must have been in a mood. The bus driver had to drop off kids about halfway down the road. There were no other kids to be dropped off down the road, so she would turn around in the last delivery's driveway and go back the other way towards the rest of the route. This time we decided to help guide her way back into the driveway because there were a couple cars in the pathway. We kept looking out the back of the bus where we were sitting and kept motioning with hand gestures to keep coming back, as she intensely looked in the large mirror in the bus for guidance as to making the turn around. Until "CRUNCH." The bus hit a car parked in the driveway. The large female bus driver nervously undid her seatbelt and exited the bus to survey the damage she did to the car in the driveway. We roared with laughter at the spectacle, until the bus driver approached the door back to the bus in which time, we became silent. She gave us a look that could kill and without a sound, she proceeded to continue with the route. I don't know if she left a note or not, but I would be very angry if I were the home owner and came home to find my car had been backed into by a bus. She proceeded to torment us in the following weeks, by kicking us of for shallow reasons. I'm sure I was kicked off the bus, but I don't really remember. We decided to take a stand! One summer night weekend, while school was still in session, we gathered at a friend's house and came up with a plan to get back at her once and for all! We devised that we would ride our bikes about 3 miles, one way to the bus driver's house and give her a "treatment." A treatment would consist of just simply toilet papering the trees heavily, but it was going to be a treatment plus! On the designated night, probably a Saturday, at least 2 people and myself, road our bikes the three miles to her house. We approached the house in the dead of night, probably about one or two am, when everyone was fast asleep and proceeded to do the following: we toilet papered the house EXTREMELY heavily, we let the air out of the vehicle tires. We didn't slash the tires, just let the air out. We took shredded newspapers and spread them all over the yard. This yard had very large boulders as landscaping, so we rolled the boulders around the yard to different spots. There were metal posts that held fencing together. We somehow removed the posts and stuck them around the yard. After our raid, we road back the three miles to our individual houses and went to sleep. The following Monday, I seem to remember all of us gathered at one stop and entered the bus together. We had huge grins on our faces as we entered the bus. The bus driver was just glaring at us as we marched to where we were to sit on the bus. The rest of the ride was rather uneventful. It was probably about a week later when we noticed signs up around the high school that read something like: "REWARD For the vandals who vandalized at "the bus driver address" Or information on the car that was driven." We were floored! We were shuddering! Luckily, we did not brag about what we had done. As for the car referenced in the reward, only one of the persons involved had a driver's license, so the angry party just assumed we drove the long way to the site of the event. So that probably saved us. People that didn't have anything to do with it were taking credit for it, which was fine by us! I remember I didn't tell my mother what we were doing the night of the so-called "crime" Back then, sometimes I would say, "A bunch of us are going to hang out around the neighborhood," and then go out. Parents were more lenient on letting their kids out back then. And after the reward and hunt was on for us, I told my mother, if anything happened, you didn't know I had gone out, I was trying to protect my parents from liability. I thought she should just go along with the fact that she didn't know anything about it if we were caught! Luckily, nothing ever became of it. We all grew up. Got our drivers licenses and no longer had to ride the bus to school. I think we dodged a bullet on that one. I think that was the last time I ever toilet papered a house again.

I didn't consider this dangerous at the time, but it could have really injured the person a lot worse, but it is still something I did.

One fine spring day I was out shooting my new BB pistol. I remember it was a C02 powered pistol. It required a C02 cartridge for it to be able to work. So, after you placed the cartridge in the pistol, you had a limited time before the air ran out and you could not shoot the gun. I was target practicing around the front yard, shooting at anything and I was getting bored. I went over to the side of my parent's garage to look for more areas to shoot, when I noticed a neighbor boy riding by on the road. I took careful aim at this person and fired the BB pistol. Assuming I missed the target, yet again, I hung my head in shame and walked back into my home and bedded down for the night.

The next day I got on the bus that picked us up every day. I walked to the back of the bus where I usually sat, because I was older and able to sit back there according to the unwritten rules of the bus. When we got to the end of our road, a family that lived at the end of the road boarded the bus. I was not even thinking of the day that I had shot my BB gun. I didn't realize it at the time, but the person I had shot at sat down next to me. He said, "Hey," were you shooting a gun yesterday?" I said, "Yes, how did you know that"? He said, "Well, I was riding my bike past your house yesterday and I think you shot me!" "That can't be," I replied back. He said, "As I was riding by your house, I saw you, holding a gun, the next thing I know, I feel a stinging sensation in my arm after I heard a "Pop" back at your house. "I think you shot at me on purpose." I said, "No, I would never do that," lying through my teeth. "I don't believe you." He said and that was it. I had shot at someone, with a BB pistol and hit him. I played dumb to the end. I can write this today, because the person I shot has passed away. Hopefully my endeavor had nothing to do with his passing many years later.

There was a neighbor that lived at the end of the road that I grew up on that used to keep soda in a kiddy pool loaded with ice. Maybe because they were farmers? Maybe they liked to work out in the fields all day and enjoy a nice cold soda pop at the end of the day. It was a thing for us local hoodlums to practice our ninja skills every weekend to go up to the farmhouse and take soda or two from this place. They even kept it right outside their front door. Sometimes we would sneak right up to their front door and take it. We kind of made it a right of passage to be able to do this. We would meet out in the field, out in front of the house around midnight and make our way up to the house. And it's not like these people were asleep. They seemed to stay up until the long hours of the morning. There were always lights on and shining all over.

We just seemed to stay in the shadows, just like Ninjas, creep up onto the porch and steal whatever pop there was sitting there. We did this during our teen-age years. Once we had car privileges, why would we do such ignorant things?

On a different note, dangerous can mean something quite different. It can be something you don't even really see. I remember working with some great people. Some I am still friends with to this day and one that was even my Best Man in my wedding named Pete. And another friend I met at Infrasource, one of the finest gentlemen I have ever known was a gentle giant. Lloyd was his name. He was a tall and wide person and looked like he could tear you apart with his teeth, but he was the nicest guy you could meet. Working with him, I got to know him and what he was about. He had no problem working 12 hours a day or more and when he was in your presence, you seemed to really listen to what he had to say. We would be at the local gathering place and I would ask, "Where is Lloyd?" And Pete would reply, "He is still at work." I would ask with a very confused "why?" Pete would reply, even more agitated, "Because he is an idiot!" As I think back on this, I know Lloyd would approve, because he told it like it is.

Unfortunately, this person is now diseased. He worked all his life and was a "company man." But he didn't get to see the fruits of his labors. He had contracted cancer. And while he battled it with the might of a bull, we all knew he had, he just did not win the fight.

Lloyd was a very well liked guy and I was disappointed at his funeral that more of the people he knew did not come to pay their respects. I remarked to Pete about it and made known my dissatisfaction about this and he agreed. I remember thinking, working yourself to death is no way to live. I'm sure if Lloyd could respond, he would have a witty way to respond! I really miss the guy!

Now, since working here in Detroit and staying here day after day, I can't say it has been crime free. I came back to the hotel one-summer afternoon and I noticed the road to the parking lot of the hotel I stayed at was blocked by police officers. I pulled up and was greeted by a police officer. He asked, "Where are you going?" I told him over to the hotel, which I was staying at. He said, "Go ahead." I later found out that there had been a shooting 2 hrs earlier at the hotel next door to where I was staying. It was a lover's triangle type of thing. So, yes, it is not the greatest area to be staying in, but this is my living area for the last two years.

A rather funny story told to me by my Grandfather when he was on the Ann Arbor police force back in the 1960's or 1970's was when he got a call about a couple of vehicles involved in an accident. He arrived on the scene and noticed two individuals standing by their cars. One car had rear-ended another. He spoke with the individual in the front car first. My Grandfather made sure he was not need of medical attention. The individual said he was stopped at a traffic light and the second car did not stop in time and rear-ended him. He then approached the gentleman in the second car that had failed to stop and had hit the front car.

My Grandfather observed an Asian man that looked rather frazzled. My Grandfather asked the man if he needed medical attention. The man stood silent starring at my Grandfather who was dressed in his full police uniform. My Grandfather asked him again, "Are you hurt? Do you need an ambulance?" The man said something in Chinese that my Grandfather didn't understand. "Do you speak English?" my Grandfather asked. The Chinese man nodded. "What happened here?" My Grandfather asked. The Chinese man replied very rapidly "I rav torrison." My Grandfather starred at the man puzzled. Seeing that there was a language barrier, my Grandfather said to the Chinese man, "Take your time, calm down and very slowly tell me again what happened." The Chinese man said very slowly "I tied to sop, but I have "corrision". The Chinese man said again slightly faster, "I have corrison weet car in front." My Grandfather realizing the man was trying to say "collision" responded with a laugh "You had a corrision alright!" My Grandfather wrote the man a fail to stop ticket and after the scene was cleared, rode on to the next call.

Some of our times are dangerous, but they can be a funny sort of danger.

CHAPTER 9
BAND DAZE

Many people decide at some point they want to play in a rock band. This usually happens at a young age, when the world is at your feet! The thought of the fame, fortune, women and everything else is quite enticing. Most of this fades when people see that it actually takes HOURS of practice, giving up your life and providing the will to commit to what it takes to actually succeed to anything that remotely resembles a band.

I decided to start playing and learning music after seeing the Oliver Stone movie "The Doors." I guess I felt a lonely, darkness with myself, as did Jim Morrison of the doors. So, I started writing down words in the form of feelings and then started writing these feelings down as lyrics. And somehow, I guess through hanging out with friends, I met a person named Todd who played drums. He invited me over, and we hung out. And as this was going on, he was trying his drumming with other musicians. I currently was just a "watcher." I consider a "watcher" a person who was there in the room while the band was playing, taking it all in. Sort of groupie. After a matter of a few practices, one of the guitarists said, when there was no one to sing, "Do you sing." I said, "Never tried." I grabbed the microphone and probably butchered whatever song I was singing. After the song, the guitarist said, "You can be the singer." I guess he thought I was decent enough. So, from that time forward I sang. I also started teaching myself guitar.

We practiced whenever we could, in this old farmhouse/party house. I practiced with many people there in that old farmhouse, as well as did plenty of partying. This was originally a farmhouse owned by a lady, who was apparently short, because the lights in the house seemed to be hanging lower than normal. On one occasion, there were a few people there at the farmhouse, partying of course and everyone kept "accidentally" walking into the lights hanging from the ceiling. A couple people kept purposely banging their heads into the low-hanging light fixtures. Everyone was laughing of course, except Todd who owned the home, he was afraid that something was going to get broke, and for a good reason. There were always drunken people there at the house, and they were always spilling drinks on the carpet. But this carpet looked like it may have been the original carpet put in when the house was built in probably 1930. It was flattened down, from all the traffic walking on it over the years, and there were so many discolored spots everywhere on the carpet, all through the house!

On occasions, there was a guy there, who was a bit slow. It happened to be the same person from earlier in school. Named Marvin. He was there just hanging out, as we all did. At some point, a muscular friend of ours, noticed a rather large dust bunny on the floor, I swear it was the size of a dime. I guess it told of the cleaning habits of the house owner. The muscular guy grabbed the rather slow fellow and proceeded to push his face down by the dust bunny. The slow fellow "Marvin" struggled trying to avoid touching the dust bunny as the rest of us just laughed. Finally, after a few minutes, this wore off and the person was let up. I feel sorry now, having witnessed this and finding humor in it.

I briefly took guitar lessons from a guy that took guitar lessons from Cub Koda, an Ann Arbor/Detroit area musician, known for many hits, including "Smoking in the Boys Room." I learned what I could from this person and soon ended the lessons after realizing that the best way to learn how to become a good musician is from practicing with a live band. I took the things I learned and put them into a live setting. Eventually, I grew better than playing with the people at the farmhouse and branched out and met musicians more of the caliber I was at, and started my venture on playing in what I consider to be real bands, and playing actual paying gigs.

There are wonderful times called "tryouts" that people do to get into bands. I really didn't have to do many of these. I only remember one in particular. I went to try out for a singing and playing rhythm guitar position in a band. Right off the bat, when I was tuning the guitar and getting a sound level on my guitar, the lead guitarist said, "Whoa, cut down on the chainsaw"! He was commenting on the distortion of my guitar. Meaning the "crunch" of the guitar. I turned down the distortion level to "calm" the lead guitarist, but I just think he didn't like me. We played "Sympathy for the Devil" by the Rolling Stones and "You Shook Me All Night Long" by AC/DC, after about an hour the lead guitarist took off his guitar, said, "Thanks for stopping by," and walked out of the room. The other members in the band really liked my way of belting out the vocals. And they certainly didn't mind the "chainsaw" guitar distortion! I think we even played a song or two without the lead guitarist, but ultimately, I was never called back. The lead guitarist probably owned the PA equipment and held the rest of the band hostage as far as decisions over whom played with that band. The guitarist sucked anyway. I have played with way better!

It's hard to play in a small-time local band. I did this from about 1995- 2021, in many different bands, with many different players, until about 2007, in which case we were the same players until I hung up the music for good in 2021. Back in the 1990's, a band I was in played around the Detroit suburbs, out in the country area bars, parties, housewarming parties, graduation or two, and at least 1 wedding that I remember. Anywhere that would let us play. I think the most people I played in front of, was about 300 and the least amount of people was six. This place that we had 300 people at, we were billed with a wrestling bear. People would pay a fee and if they could pin the bear, they would win a cash prize of $1000.00. We played a set for about 45 minutes, and then the bear wrestling happened. In which case the bar emptied to the parking lot. I do not think anyone pinned the bear. After the bear wrestling, pretty much everyone left. So, it was safe to say that everyone was there to watch the bear wrestling, which was more of a draw then our band! Pretty bad when a bear does better than the band!

We played a place called "Studio Lounge" in Westland, MI. It's no longer there, but this was the happening place at the time. We played this place a few times as the back up band, which means you are the band that goes on before the main headlining band for the night. I think we got a guaranteed $25.00 for the band for 1 set, which is about 45 minutes of music.

The band would drive there, set up the equipment, which seemed to take us about an hour and the play our 45-minute set. We then would take all the equipment down after the set, which seemed to take about 20 minutes and then leave for the night, after getting paid. We talked Studio Lounge into making our band the headlining band. So, our name, which was "Jaded Wing" at the time, was up on the marquee, beaming the letters of our name in the neon, out into the night, to be seared into the brains of everyone who passed by the place.

The only drawback was the headliner was paid from the door, which was how many people were there to see you. We played a great show. There was a moderate amount of people at the establishment that night. We felt we really "rocked it." So, when it came time to collect the pay for the show, needless to say it was a total disappointment. What we didn't know was that they asked people as they came in the bar was who of the usual two to three bands they were there to see and they split up the money that way. I want to say we made $6.75 that night. Total. And we were a four-piece band.

Another time, we played a place in Adrian, MI. where we were also paid by the door. And we had to rely on someone that worked there named "Swinger" to collect the money from the people coming in. This guy was a real piece of work. Overweight, sort of pushing himself around when he walked, and had a cigar sticking out of his mouth that he chewed on all night like a toothpick. We played both Friday and Saturday. So, Friday night, we had a decent night, there was a good amount of people. I think we made around $300.00, so we were hoping for a better night on Saturday.

So, when we played Saturday, it was nuts. There were even more people there than Friday night, and they were in party mode. Yelling and screaming. Laughing, dancing, people having fun. We thought we had it made. We were going to make so much that night, because the place was packed in comparison to the night before. So, at the end of the night, after we had the sweat rolling off our skin as we tore down the equipment, and our eyes dry like desert sand from cigarette smoke (you could smoke in the bars, back in the day). We were weak and weary from the show and loading equipment. It was finally time for that moment, that wonderful moment. That moment when you get paid. And we knew we did a good job. All the hard work would finally pay off. All the running around on stage, all the loud music, not to mention, all the loading the equipment, taking it there, unloading it, setting it up, playing the show, and then reloading it back up, YES, it was time to get paid. And we got $200.00 for the night. Wait a minute, back up the trolley, $200.00? But that was $100.00 less than the night before and there were more people here tonight. Yes folks, this is the type of thing you can expect if you want to play in a band. Needless to say, we did not play there again.

Another place we played frequently was "Dino's Dugout" in Milan, MI. This was the same place that we played with the bear wrestling that I talked about earlier. They had a banquet room that they had the bands play in that was very large and could seat many. So, the first time we played there, before the bear wrestling gig, we really wanted to impress the owner of the place. We set up and did a sound check. Now I do not know who they have had their previously, but I think the waitresses were thinking "Oh, another crappy band we have to serve drinks to." But as we played the first notes and the guitars ripped into the air with sound, they were surprised and immediately got up on top of the bar and started to dance with the music. I had never had this happen before, so it was a very excellent surprise.

One of the things I remember from playing at Dino's Dugout, was that we had put up our banner that had our bands name on it. We had put it up with masking tape (I think the band was named Blazing Sky's), (yes, we changed the name to Sky's, when people became confused and thought we were a skiing band!) and apparently the tape on the banner was very sticky. So, when it came time to tear it back down, the owner "George," an Arabic gentleman, happened to be standing there as the lead guitarist in the band named Tony was taking it down off the wall.

The lead guitarist ripped the banner down off the wall, the paint came off with it. "Look what you are doing to my wall," George yelled out. "I'm really sorry," Tony responded as he continued to rip more paint off the wall. We just continued to laugh about it as we continued to tear down the equipment.

A different time at "Studio Lounge," the club located in Westland, MI. After a show, we were tearing down the equipment. The lead guitarist had got into an argument with the man running the sound during the show over how his guitar sounded while we were playing, so he was not in the best of moods. It was cold out that night. You could see our breath, as well as the exhaust of the vehicles parked right near the back door of the building for loading. We had the door propped open, so we could quickly load the equipment. The soundman came out and said angrily, "Hurry up and get loaded, the fumes are getting into the building." As he turned and walked back inside, Tony, the lead guitarist, standing in the doorway, turned towards the soundman as he walked back into the building and made motions with his hands, as if he were waving the fumes into the building.

I can say that we had seen some wild things, while playing in a band that people have done, while obviously intoxicated. There was a guy one time that said we were playing too quiet. Now most places we played; we were almost always told to turn the volume down. But a few places did not care. And this guy said we were too quiet. It just so happened to be a place where we were cranking the volume up! Our ears were literally ringing after the show. So, during the show, this guy decides to stick his head in the speaker, while we are playing. I guess he did this to make sure it was working? He had to be deafened. I cannot imagine, as loud as it was, to put my head in there. He was out of his mind! I do not remember what he said, after we took a break, I just remember his attempt to help fix our sound that night!

Another thing we saw was a lot of people who vomited. There was plenty of vomiting. Vomiting on the tables, vomiting on the bar, vomiting in the parking lot, vomiting in the bathroom, and vomiting on themselves. Plenty of VOMITING! The point of this story you ask? Well, it must be told.

A woman, who had been drinking at the bar for a while, was tearing it up on the dance floor at one of our shows. And she was one of those types, that could dance, while holding a drink in her hand, and while still dancing, was able to take a drink from the glass, while still dancing, without seeming to spill one drop. And when the drink was gone, get another, and repeat the process for a few hours. At one point, a female friend of ours, happened to be in the woman's bathroom just at the moment that this dancing wonder was in there to release some of the alcohol she had downed, but instead of letting it out the natural way, she vomited it all out.

After losing a few pounds of alcohol by barfing, she walked to the mirror, fixed her hair, washed her hands, and walked out of the bathroom! Not even a mouth rinse to get the stomach/alcohol mix flavor out of her mouth. So, about 20 minutes later, after we start another set of music, this woman is back out on the dance floor. What a trooper! She is like our best guest of the night. So, we heard what happened in the bathroom from our female friend, and were amazed that she was still going, and yes, she had a new drink in hand for our next set. But what we witnessed next; we are barely able to keep playing.

One unwitting gentleman decided he was going to move in on this lone woman on the dance floor. His courage built as he moved closer and closer to her. He showed his moves to the music and she accepted his invitation. Pretty soon they were one, dancing together. It was a fast song, but they were moving, as they were one, right next to each other. Then it happened. This poor guy decided he was going to passionately kiss this woman while in the moment of this seductive dance. We were laughing, as we were trying not to get sick, all the while wondering if the guy could taste the mix of drinks, stomach bile, and perhaps other men's saliva, as they were in their moment. We kept playing, not missing a note of music. This is a memory I don't forget to this day!

The places you play expect you to have a following. Which means to bring people into the establishment, fill seats, and put butts in the chairs! You can tell everyone you know, HEY, I'm playing at this place, come see me, but most of the people you invite, will not show up. I made a lot of recordings of our shows during the time, so there is a record of some of them. While playing in a band, this was about 2009, we were playing at local place, in Pinckney, MI., which by the way, we did well at.

So, we went onstage, which was about 9:30 PM, which was usually pretty standard at the smaller circuit places. It may have been the first song of the night, I am not sure, and immediately, a couple people came out on the dance floor. Now, this is unusual because NO ONE wants to be the first person out. They do not want to break the dance floor seal. But here we were, the colored lights changing and caressing your eyes, the music, beating into your soul, and these people were out there at the first song.

Now, I, being the one who is more the person who makes sure that everything sounds good and everything looks good and everyone is getting the show we want them to experience, am not seeing the warning signs. I am not noticing one of the persons stumbling. I am not noticing one of the persons having trouble standing up as they are dancing. This female individual, mis-stepped, lost her balance or just plain passes out and falls forward towards the jukebox and about put her head through the front of it where the speakers are located. The whole band just laughed as the person was picked up or she was more dragged of the dance floor and I'm sure as this is happening, I made a comment, "Jeez, 9:30 and already bombed," pointing out that it was only 9:30 and this person was already blitzed. I was usually known for making a comment like that, in that type of situation.

There are other times playing out where family members attended, like where my uncle

Mike and Aunt Sheila, along with their sons Andy, Geoffry and Sean, came out to see us, and it happen to be my Uncle Mike's Birthday, so we sang him Happy Birthday rock band style. We played "Happy Birthday" by The Beatles. He said, "I can truly say no one has done that for me before." Throughout my time playing, we always did birthdays this way. I feel that singing the same old traditional birthday song is so lame. I made sure every band I was in, that we knew how to play "Birthday" by The Beatles.

In the later years, we played a biker club called the Ghost Riders. Some of the events they held were thing such as take bets on a motorcycle that was throttled wide open and see how long it could go before the engine would blow. They had a mechanical bull-riding event, to see who could stay on it the longest. I seem to remember that they always wanted women to ride the bull ride topless. They would see whose bike would do the best burnout, which would produce a lot of smoke. It was a fun time, but it seemed like almost every time we played there, it would rain.

One of the last times we played there, we were playing Riders on the Storm by "The Doors" and it started to pour down rain. What few people there were left in attendance by this time, started crowding in as close as they could inside the covered areas. The area where the bands played were luckily covered, but they still leaked from the roof. Rich, the drummer, my brother Kent the guitarist and I continued to play while it was absolutely poring outside the covered area. The band finished the song and as I was playing the final notes of the song, water was dripping onto the keyboard and I can only assume it was dripping all over the other band mates equipment. The people chanted "MORE," "MORE," "MORE," but I said, "It's pouring, it's time to go!" At which time we ended the concert. I liked playing the outside concerts, but this place, we always seemed to have sound problems. The last time we left from there, it was a muddy mess!

We played a Halloween party one-year and it happens to be at a home that was proclaimed to be a 1 Million-Dollar home. This home, maybe in the 1970's was worth 1 million dollars, but in 2014 when we were there it was quite outdated and not worth the money proclaimed. The drummer Rich, my brother Kent and myself played our hearts out. It was probably one of our better shows. A pizza was ordered at some point and when the pizza arrived, there is a recording of it.

While still playing, we announced that the pizza had arrived and we played a song that we made up on the spot and played called "The Pizza Song" I have a recording of it. Later after the party was over and we were tearing the equipment down, a couple showed up to the party that was heavily influenced by drugs and alcohol. If I remember right, the guy was dressed as a priest. So, as we were loading the equipment, a fight sort of broke out between the priest and one of the people that was with the band that was helping to load the equipment. I have no idea to this day what the fight was about. I think the priest was just so gone at that point, that he would have fought anyone in his path. What I saw was the priest standing there with our roadie stiffening up his posture. He was making fists and being threatening. The roadie happened to have a metal flashlight in his hand that he was using to help light the area as we were loading the vehicles. As the out of control priest made his way closer to the roadie and threw a punch, the roadie moved out of the way and retaliated by hitting the man at least once in the head with the flashlight. That is about all I saw. I heard screaming, followed by the man dressed as a priest rolling on the ground and the roadie and his girlfriend kicking him.

After it was over, the priest disappeared into the night with his girlfriend. I noticed that there was some blood on the front of my vehicle. I asked the roadie, "Hey man, what is up with this"? He said, "I'm sorry, I will pay to have it washed off." I told him it wasn't a big deal. The following day, I had heard that the man dressed as a priest had went to the hospital and he had a few staples put into his head. I guess he should have not messed with our crew that night!

Something I got asked all the time, while playing a show was someone asking, "Hey, I play guitar, can I sit in with the band and play a song?" Most of these people, played a few guitar riffs, but didn't really know a song all the way through. And also, we didn't know most of the people that were asking this. Number one, you risk the band being embarrassed if someone were to sit in that really sucked. Number two, you are trusting someone with your equipment and not knowing if they will decide to go with a "WHO" maneuver and break something. Even on accident. I usually said, "No, we can't because of insurance purposes." And that usually worked. One time a guy said, "You guys are just egomaniacs and don't want to take a chance on someone showing you up!" That really wasn't it. We or I guess I should say I, didn't trust anyone to sit in that we didn't know. Now if we did know them? It was not a problem. I actually have a few recordings with someone we knew sitting in with the band.

Anytime I went to see a band, I never asked to sit in. If I sat in, it was because I was asked to. One time we were watching a band at a place called Garlin's, which was in Manchester, Michigan. I noticed the soundboard for the band and one of the channels was overloading. This meant that one of the inputs of the vocals or the instruments was coming into the channel too much. At a break time, I told the vocalist for the band of the flaw that was happening, because it can affect the sound. He said, "Thanks man!" and proceeded to ask how I knew about the sound for the band. I told him I was in a band too. He said, "Why don't you sit in?" I said, "That would be cool!" When the band went back on, we rocked out "Roadhouse Blues" by The Doors. Then for the second song, we played "Rock and Roll" by Led Zeppelin.

I remember the place seemed to go wild. I really felt good with this band. They all said thanks and I walked back to my table. As I did, a couple people said to me "hey, you should be singing for this band!" "You sound better than their singer!" If only they had told the band members that, maybe my band times I went through would be different. It takes a certain bunch of people together to be really good, you can have good players, but if they don't have a gelling chemistry together, it will not work. This was not the only time I was told I should be singing for a band I sat in with.

Another time I sat in with a band that played around the circuit and became quite popular. We even played together one time in my parent's garage to see if we all could play together with the current members of each band.. The leader of the other band was very forward about what he wanted, so he would always be the leader and would always decide the direction of his band, so we never went farther than my parent's garage. But we still remained friends as bands do. If I showed up at this bands show, he would have me come up and do a song or two.

One of the times I remember, the band was playing locally and they asked me to come up and sing. They played "Honky Tonk Blues" by the Rolling Stones and we sounded really good I thought. I said to the lead guitarist, "Hey, lets play Yellow Ledbetter." I knew they played this song, because I had heard them do it before at a different show and my band did it and I thought I sang it very well. "Ok, let's do it." He said. After a few moments of directing the rest of the band to play the desired song, the cymbals rang out on the opening note. I belted out the song as if my life depended on it. We did a great version of the song, in my opinion. I shook hands with all of the band members and walked of the stage with the crowd cheering. This band always seemed to have a good crowd. I always wished any of my bands had this type of attendance. As I walked back towards where I was sitting, I was stopped about two or three times by people congratulating me on a fine performance. It really made me feel good. It is quite something to have people glorifying you for something. Once again, at least two of the people said, "You should be singing for this band." I replied, "Tell the band!" Of course, nothing ever came of it. I truly believe there were at least three times that I played with a band other than my own, that I could have excelled with. It was just the chemistry. And maybe it would have been different if you were on a more intimate setting such as rehearsal. But it was very exciting a few times to actually feel like a rock star!

CHAPTER 10
SIMPLY HANGING OUT

All through life, everyone hangs out, whether it is at a party, a get together, church function, or even a date. It can be two people to hundreds of people. While most of the time you are doing this, you are burning time of your life, with no gain. But if you are lucky enough, sometimes you can gain knowledge by doing this. It can give you advantages in making good decisions.

On the other hand, it can also lead to EXTREMELY bad decisions. Listening to other people's stories can give you ideas on how to make your own living situation a better environment. For instance, if you are hanging out with a fitness enthusiast, you may be prone to live a healthier life. If you are in the company of people who choose to partake in the party atmosphere, you may find yourself in trouble. You can learn a lot by listening to people's stories. Hopefully, you are in good company that will lead you on an honest, healthy, and wholesome path.

At this time, I had obtained my driver's license, I decided to drive up North to visit my Paternal Grandmother. Sort of a victory celebration of driving, going up North to Central Lake, Michigan, a drive I was familiar with but had never made myself. After reaching my destination and talking for some time with my Grandmother, she placed a phone call to one of her Sister's (my great Aunt Barbara).

After a short hello, my Grandmother said to the person on the other end of the phone, "Hey, guess who is here?" My Aunt Barbara had no idea. "Chad is!" my grandma Young exclaimed! I went on to talk to my Aunt Barbara for a bit. During that time, I may not have thought much about it, but thinking now, I feel they made it out like it was so wonderful to be talking to me. They made me feel like I was some sort of famous person. That is just the way they were. They were all great people who loved their family.

Later in life, when Aunt Barbara passed away, we were sitting in the church, listening to the service. The person speaking mentioned how Aunt

Barbara always sat in the congregation where me and my immediate family happened to be sitting. I happened to feel this coldness go through me just after the speaker said that as if a cold air vent was blowing directly on me. It lasted only a few seconds. I was sure it was my Aunt touching me. Sort of her way of saying goodbye. I do not think anyone else felt it, but I know I did. It may have been my imagination, but I am positive I felt something!

My Grandpa Hughes was a great storyteller. Or maybe I am simply good at visualizing what he was saying. The following story happened a few years before he joined the army and went on to fight in World War two. He told how he was friends with Harry Bennett, a former boxer and ex-Navy sailor, who was an executive at Ford Motor Company during the 1930s and 1940s. He was best known as the head of Ford's internal security.

My Grandfather was Golden Gloves champion in the early thirties, so he had that in common with Harry. He met Harry because my Grandfather's brother was dating Harry's daughter, Trudie Bennett. My Grandfathers brother and Trudie Bennett ended up running away together. It was a whole news story when it happened back in Ann Arbor, Michigan, in 1938. They thought she was kidnapped because of Harry's involvement with the mob and his high profile in the Ford Motor Company.

A story was run in the local newspaper about what thought to be a kidnapping. Later the two turned up. I suppose after they read the story, and they both were fine. My Grandfathers story about Harry Bennett and his time spent with him was remarkably interesting. Harry Bennett worked as Henry Ford's head of security and had a reputation for using whatever means he needed to use to get things done. If that included violence, so be it. But Harry was always a pleasant host at home according to my Grandfather. He really felt humbled when Harry got him a sweater one Christmas. I myself would have been ecstatic to be rubbing elbows with such a person, but to my Grandfather, it was just another day in life. He told me how Harry showed him around his house, located on Geddes Road, in Ann Arbor, Michigan, which is there to this day. He said Harry led him to a bathroom that had a secret door that led downstairs to a room underneath the house.

My Grandfather said he had an alligator down in the secret area under the home. Now I have no idea why a person would have an alligator, but being it was someone like Harry Bennett, I am wondering if it was to help get rid of bodies. My Grandfather said there were all kinds of secret doors and rooms in the house. The doors were there, so if Harry needed to make a quick escape, for whatever reason, he would be able to. My Grandfather said Harry always employed the largest ex-felons, just out of prison as his personal bodyguards. Whenever he visited Harry, there were these huge guys around for Harry's protection, although from what I have heard and read about Harry, he could handle himself and was not someone to mess with. But my Grandfather said Harry's bodyguards were always nice to him, and Harry himself always treated him like a son.

Now, let me clarify, I never doubted anything my Grandfather told me. I never thought for a second, that he over embellished a story to make it seem more interesting. I just found the whole story about Harry Bennett interesting, so I did some reading and research on him. The stories my Grandfather told me about Harry Bennett's house and the secret rooms were all true, because I have found recent stories online, about interviews with the current owners of the property, and they were showing the interviewer all of the secret rooms throughout the house. So, for my Grandfather, hanging out with Harry was just as simple as spending time with a friend. But in reality, it was spending time with an alleged criminal.

Hanging out with people can sometimes be fun, but there is always the chance for it to turn sour! While working at the Chelsea Retirement home, one of the supervisors I worked for had a party. And a lot of the employees I worked with were there. One of my co-workers who was there was plenty past her limit, exclaimed to the department manager in a slurred manner, while stumbling in place where she stood, "I could tell you how much food Chad has taken out of that kitchen!" I just froze. I started to try to think of something to say, to downplay the statement. But before I could say anything, the manager, who was pretty lit up herself, said to the employee, "I think you need another drink"! Everyone just laughed, and luckily the situation was never brought up again at the party, or back at work. Lucky I was, once again! Hanging out could have turned into a disaster!

Later in life, when I was much older Grandfather, my parents went away on vacation, so I was going over to take care of their house. Feed the cat, get the mail, whatever needed to be done. I believe before my parents left, the next door neighbor had invited them to a party at his house he was having that weekend. They told him they would be away, but I would be there taking care of the house. Apparently, he told them to let me know I was welcome to come to the party. I bet the gentleman regrets that decision now! Of course, I took him up on his offer!

First, let me say I thought it was a great time. A nice property to visit and had fun talking to everyone. The neighbor had catered in a gentleman that barbecued the best pork and chicken. I'm not a barbecue fan, but it was very good. My Aunt Lowene and Uncle Jeff were there briefly and even the neighborhood farmer that lived down the road came down for the party. Now this neighbor that lived down the road from my mom and dad loved to socialize. You could go buy eggs from him, something that should take 5-10 minutes, but you would be there talking with him for an hour, and he would never let you leave. This is a true story, my uncle Jeff went down there to buy eggs and after one and a half hours, my Aunt Lowene finally went looking for him and found him at the farmer's house conversing.

Do not get me wrong, he was a very nice man. The farmer went the longest time without a TV, and finally after one year his family got him one. I ran into him at a local store and talked to him briefly. I said, "I heard your got yourself a new TV." "How are you liking it?" He responded in a robotic like fashion "I'm not liking it at all!" Shocked, I replied, "Why is that?" He said in response, just like it was a profoundly serious matter, not even a smile, "It's interfering with my sleep!" As I laughed, he cracked a smile. He was just a nice guy with a dry sense of humor and a good neighbor. He was in his usual form at the party.

I remember the party probably started about 3 pm on a warm summer night and went to who knows what time that night. I remember seeing this farmer neighbor in the afternoon. I think it may have been one of the best parties he had ever been to. So yes, I had been drinking all night, as were most people there at the party. I remember talking to the hosts son after he played some guitar for everyone, telling him he was particularly good, he just needed a band to back him. I do not know, maybe I had been a little overbearing in my explanation. I meant well, but he may have taken it as negative. I don't think I really got out of hand, but then again do most people who have been drinking.

So, a few weeks after the party, I was visiting Mom and Dad, and they had spoken with the neighbor, just as neighbors do from time to time. My parents asked their neighbor how his party had gone a few weeks back. He said, "Very good". "Apparently, your son had a really good time". I have no idea what that means. It could be the following.

The host of the party had a nice Corvette, and I happen to love Corvettes. I kept asking him jokingly if I could drive it. If I could take it real slow down the road. I was of course joking! I kept asking him like a child and he kept saying NO every time I asked. Maybe he thought I was serious. My Mom says sometimes when they talk to him, he talks about "All the hell I raised" at his party. My Mom said, "I don't even want to know what you did!". I personally do not even know what I did, I sometimes wonder what I may have done.

At this same party I met a couple of women in their 50's or 60's and we started talking about the Wizard of Oz. I'm sure I brought up the facts of the movie. I don't remember how the conversation started, but I was amazed at the fact that neither of them had seen the 1939 spectacular movie! It seemed, at this point in time, like it was my WHOLE LIFES meaning, was to tell these two poor women who I had never met before, that their only purpose in life at this point was to see the Wizard of Oz! I really felt that they should see the film! They may have looked at me like some crazy, delusional individual, but I really felt that they should have seen this movie at this point in their life!

This story is second hand. I didn't witness it; it is just one of those ones you hear. I have worked for a company, for many years, that installs gas pipes into the ground. I had heard that a couple of crews had got together one night after work and were sitting around talking and drinking, when someone got the grand idea to have a sword fight with two backhoes.

For those who may not know what a backhoe is, it is a tractor with a bucket on the front of it, and arm with a small bucket on the back of it. The bucket in the back digs the holes in the ground. So, some workers got a couple of backhoes together and had a fight. They had a sword match of sorts. So, there they are. Two backhoes backed up to each other. Then, maybe after someone said "GO," they knocked the arms and small buckets on the back of the machine together, like a "sword fight." I don't know how the match was to determine the winner. I doubt, knowing some of the people that work for these types of companies even think that far ahead.

I guess they did this, until, somehow, one of the digging machines toppled over the other machine over onto its side. I am not sure how they got it upright. They must have attached a chain to it and pulled it back over. I would hope both operators of the machines lost their jobs.

Another story is about a foreman that had received a brand-new truck, as did the entire foreman with the company at that time. Back then, just as the policy is to date, the foreman was only to use the company vehicle for business purposes. Whether this was just after work or on a weekend this story still constitutes as bad judgment. It was a harsh Michigan winter. Snow, frigid winds, but people still like to ice fish. And this foreman was one of those people.

He took himself and his son out on the ice for a day of ice fishing. And when I say, "out on the ice," I mean out the ice, with the brand-new company vehicle! This individual drove the truck out onto the frozen ice. I do not know how long they were out on the spot, how far out on the lake they were, or if they got out of the truck and set up the site for the fishing. What I do know, is the truck fell through the ice and proceeded to go to the bottom of the lake. Now, the obvious problem with this is a work truck being used beyond work hours. But the worst part of it was this person was drinking.

I am told when the truck was fished out of the lake, there were empty beer cans in the front part of the truck. And on top of that, there was all the equipment he was carrying in the truck at the time. Maybe another $5000.00 worth. Of course, this gentleman was let go from the company for the incident. I am not sure what year this happened. Maybe early 2000, but the statute of limitations for some companies are not the same as others. What do I mean by this you ask? Well, the individual involved with this was hired back with the same company. I am guessing 2017 or so this individual was hired back until he retired!

When I was younger, under the drinking age, a friend and myself had a person that we worked with that would buy us alcohol. We would usually have him buy us some beers and then we would hang out at his parent's house. Since he was supposed to be baby sitting his brothers while his parents went out until about 1 or 2:00 am in the morning, we were left to entertain ourselves how we wanted.

Our circle of friends would show up while his parents were still there, then after they left, we would break out the booze. Usually, it was just beer. It was usually harmless. We would drink a few beers, have a few laughs, then we would all go home before his parents returned. One evening, we invited the individual who bought us alcohol to our party. That night, it was Mr. M-80, the person who was buying us alcohol and myself. This night, the person brought us the beer we ordered, but he also brought liquor. Vodka was his poison. He had brought a few pints. And it was enough for the three of us. We drank it, the beer and vodka while watching music videos. I remember the three of us head banging to an AC/DC video. I do not know if we were mixing the vodka or drinking straight, but we finished a lot of it.

Mr. M-80 as we will call him, was drinking a pint of vodka all by himself. And at one point he held up the bottle, which at this time was about ¾ gone and he was trying to say that he drank ¾ quarters of the bottle, but instead it came out, "I drank 3 corners". We all laughed as he said it a couple more times. It got time to leave, so we said our good-byes and the person who bought the alcohol and my self headed out for home. Mr. M-80 didn't seem like he was really drunk, so I wasn't worried about him. And I was not drunk myself because I had not drunk that much. I got home no problem and went to bed.

The next morning after I woke up and was like any other day, I was probably sitting in my parents living room and watching television. It was probably around 1:00 in the afternoon, the phone rang, my mother answered it and said, "Chad, it's for you." I picked up the phone and it was my friend, Mr. M-80. "How are you feeling," I asked, after the party the night before. "Ok," he said. He then asked, "Hey, can you come over right now?" I replied slowly, "I guess." I drove over wondering what was going on, because I never had really been to his house during the day, it was always towards the evening.

When I arrived, I do not remember who answered the door, but I went in and sat down on the couch. His parents were in there sitting in the living room and my friend was sitting very quietly in a chair in the room. After what seemed like a few minutes of silence, his Father, who was a bulky gentleman, said, "So I heard you had some sauce here last night." I really did not know how to respond to that, so I went with my instinct and said in a shaky voice "No, I don't know what you are talking about." My friend broke in and exclaimed "Chad, I told them everything." I then confessed and answered all the questions that followed with total honesty. "Where did you guys get the alcohol?" his Father asked. And we told him, "A guy we work with." My friend's father said when they got home the night we partied there, my friend was passed out on the kitchen floor. The angry father said, "I had to kick him around to get him to wake up!" His Mom blurted out, "I'm very disappointed in you boys!"

After a few more questions I do not really remember, my friend's Father asked me for my parent's phone number, which I gave him. At that point, I guess I was allowed to leave and I headed home. I was shaking. I was caught, and my parents were going to find out. I did not know how they were going to react. I was very scared. After I got home, things seemed normal, so I knew the dreaded call had not happened yet, so, I rolled the dice and decided to tell my father what had happened and to probably expect a call from my friend's father. And then the call came. My father must have spent a half-hour or so talking with my friend's father. After the call, my Father came to me and said, "You really did it this time didn't you?" I said in a hardly audible voice "Yea." "Well." My father said in a more stern voice. "You know you have to be punished." I replied in a cowering voice, "Yes," then my Father replied in a calmer voice. "Two weeks without TV." I replied like I had just been given a life sentence, "Come on!" My father then said, "OK, 1 week." I guess going forward, I could have perceived that as weakness and used that to my advantage for any future mischief, but I think I really thought that was simply good parenting.

I made a mistake, my father hoped I had learned something from it, which I think I did. After a couple months my M-80 friend's parents let us start coming over again when they were gone. If I remember right, we may have still had a few drinks while my friends parents were gone, which I guess looking back we broke their trust again, but it was never again like the that one night that all hell broke loose. Never again like that bad night. At least not at that house again.

When I was just out of high school, a group of our friends that were hanging out at the time continued to party without a care in the world. We usually got together at a local park outside of Chelsea, MI. that was called Park Sharon. We spent many nights there just talking and drinking. Somehow, someone in the group had heard of a party at someone's house. I am not even sure where it was. My memory is not so good anymore. We found the location and we proceeded to "crash" the party. I remember, the person that lived there, his name was "Joe," but that is about it. I remember it was a genuinely nice home. It even had a swimming pool.

We met some friends of the individual who was throwing the party and explained to them that we really did not know the host and had basically trespassed. They said, "No worries," if we were not stealing anything or tearing up the place, we could stay." We hung out by the pool for the rest of the night with our small group. There is something about a pool at night for me. I love the lighted water, glistening as it moves to the beat of an unseen heartbeat. I love to sit by a pool at night and just watch the water. It is quite relaxing.

Hanging out can also be a date with someone. The first date with my now wife was a funny experience. We met on an online social media-dating site. After a couple weeks of talking back and forth, she finally got impatient with the process and gave me her phone number.

Soon after that we made a date to meet on a Sunday afternoon about 5:00 pm at the Applebee's in Ann Arbor, Michigan. (Which is no longer there, it was probably closed due to Covid). We both showed up on time as both of us were prompt and on time people. After general introductions, I followed an online dating procedure, which is to state a time you absolutely have to leave. You can use this as an escape if the date is not going good. I stated that I am a huge fan of walking dead and never missed an episode, which really was not a lie. I really did like the show walking dead. This immediately made Anna, my date think I didn't like her, because I stated a television show was more important than a date, if the date happened to run longer than expected!

I was cool as a cucumber. I liked her. She was funny, cute, dressed nice for the date. I even remember she had on a leopard skin top on. She on the other hand was so flustered and nervous during our meal that she dropped salad on her chest. She was embarrassed beyond belief. She felt much better when I explained that I put an end time on the date in case things didn't go well". But I was indeed have a wonderful time! Needless to say, after dinner we walked around the local mall and then stopped at an eatery to have some sodas. I ended up missing walking dead that night! We spent the next three years together and were married.

My wife and I were not married at the time, but while on vacation in San Francisco, I found myself wandering the streets near the docks in search of a light for my cigar. My girlfriend at the time Anna and I had a huge fight, so I left the room to give some cool off time. I asked a few passerby's alone the way if they had a light, but found no one to fill my quest. I spotted a homeless gal hanging out near a restaurant, so I told her if she had a light for my cigar, she could have all the spare change in my pocket, which was about .53 cents. She delightedly pulled out a lighter from the pocket of her cut off shorts and lit my about one inch cigar.

After getting the light I was searching for, I felt compelled to ask her about her situation, and why she was sitting outside of a restaurant by the Bay of San Francisco. She told me in her Russian accented English, that she had married an American man. He had brought her to America to live and prosper. But the man suddenly died of a heart attack. She said she was left with nothing and had to fend for herself now in America. Unfortunately, she ended up there on the dock area of San Francisco. As I sat there smoking my cigar and listening to her story, I couldn't help but feel somewhat sorry, because I could go back to my hotel room and my eventual life, while she was somewhat stuck in the life, she was in.

At some point while we were talking, an employee came out of the restaurant that we were sitting by and saw me smoking my cigar. He stated, "You can't be doing that here." He thought we were smoking drugs. I told him, "Hey man, it's just a regular cigar." He said, "Ok" and walked back into the restaurant. As the sun started to set, it began to get colder as we sat there talking about life. The woman took off her short pants right there in front of me and changed into long pants for warmth. As she stripped, I noticed tracks on her legs near her knees, and at that moment I knew I was talking to a heroin addict. About this time, a man walked up and started asking what I was doing here, and the woman exclaimed, "He gave me all of his change to light his cigar!" After a few seconds, the man sat down with us and started to talk with me. After talking for a while, the man told me his name was "Tony." We had general conversation for a while, and then when I felt comfortable with this gentleman, whom I felt, was someone running from the law, I asked him if he had ever killed someone. He said, "I don't want to answer that." I seemed to notice the man directing the woman to go off with another man and they walked down the dock end, where it was not so light.

I guessed by this time, that he was the pimp. I gave "Tony" the rest of my cigar, by now was about a ½ inch long. And he continued to smoke it, saying "Wow," this is good. This was a cigar given to me by my wife's mother, a Macadamia, and it was good. As he finished the 1/2-inch of the cigar, the Russian woman came back and sat down with us. I guess it was time to go wherever they went at that time of night. We all stood up and said our good-byes.

"Tony" said it was great to meet a person like me that did not "judge people who were down on their luck." He then ordered the Russian woman to pull up her shirt and show me her breasts, which she immediately did! I was so stunned; I did not know what to say. I just said "thanks" as I observed the small set of breasts in front of me. I watched them as they picked up their belongings and proceeded to wherever life was taking them. As I was walking back to the hotel, I thought to myself how lucky I was to not be living on the streets!

If you are ever away for work with a group of people there is usually a time or two where hanging out is involved. And if you are away from home for work for long periods of time, you get to know your co-workers and very easily begin to hangout with them. On one long stretch of working away from home, I worked with and stayed at the same hotel with a lot of fine gentlemen! Luckily all of us had our own room. But for some reason during this time all of us seemed to gravitate and congregate in one room.

The Unlucky man's name was Reed. He was a most gracious host. He never turned anyone away. I would not want people hanging out in my room every night. I remember he said he tried to be quiet one night and not answer the door as the drunk people on the outside of the door were knocking, but one of the drunks said they would kick in the door if he didn't open it, so he opened it! I would have let him kick it down and got a new room! I met a lot of nice people in that room. Construction workers are a very loyal and trustworthy bunch. There was Reed, Josh, and Randy, who was Reeds brother, Dani, who was Reed and Randy's Aunt, Brian and a very nice man with the last name Drinkwine. And this man with the unique name did not drink so he never had to live up to his name! You never know the friends you will make, the experiences you will have or even have a chance to do either unless you socialize and hang out with other people.

CHAPTER 11
OUT ON THE ROAD

People have to do certain things in life. They may have to live in a concentration camp as my Grandfather did and live under conditions that may not be suitable for human life. A person may have to give up their home to foreclosure. An individual may lose his possessions to a hurricane, tornado, or maybe a flood. There are horrible things that happen in life and depending on the time, they can vary from person to person.

I don't envy the people that have had to fight in wars, or have had to endure great obstacles in their life. I don't in any way try to value my life to those that have served in the military, or that have survived any kind of disaster that has happened more recently. Everyone goes through tough times in his or her life if they have the will to persevere.

The toughest for me has been working away from home. And I am still doing this as of this writing. While I believe that I have led an uneventful life, probably like most Americans, it may be more adventurous than others. There are some people that have never left the city or town that they grew up in!

I may not have stories that will reach out and grab you like those of a rock star or movie star and may not have the stories that my Grandfather did, but in a way, I seem to have my own set of stories that maybe some people would envy. Mostly because I have worked jobs that require traveling. Currently, to date, I have worked away from home and have spent about 5 years of my adult life living in a hotel. That means living in a hotel room and coming home on weekends for all that time.

For those people that has not done this, you have no idea what it's like. The packing and the planning. I currently pack a suitcase for the week, as well as food for the week. That means planning what to wear and what to eat for the week, and just making sure you have what you need to last for the week is an event. Remembering what you may need to replenish as far as medicine, toiletries, or any other necessities. Then once at the hotel, unpack the clothes and the food. At the end of the workweek, you pack up all the clothes and left over food for the trek home. It is reputation at it's finest. It starts to resemble a form of prison in a way. No, you are not locked up or shackled in any way, but after you miss a few summers spending time at home, you may feel very restricted. As though you're are in a form of prison.

Vacations are not the same either, because you spend your time in yet another hotel room. It's hard to enjoy a vacation like this, because sometimes you just want to stay home for a change. One way to describe this, at least for me, is that I'm in a coma. My mind is running through the motions and making my body obey and commit to motion, but there is not a soul present. The days blur together. At times I am just a zombie walking forth. Before you know it, year has gone by, then two. If you take a vacation during this year, you remember it, but it seems to be swirled together with the everyday occurrence. At least, this is how it is for me. It's a job, but the price for it seems to be rather steep. But you do get stories to remember. If you make them happen.

For our stay in Ohio, my 3 co-workers and I got to know the employees that worked at that hotel, being we were there for a year. I remember we had to clear out of the hotel in the spring because the Cleveland Browns stayed there during their training. I never saw a football star, but I saw plenty of Hummer SUV's and sports cars in the parking lot. After we finally were done with the job in Ohio, I wrote the Corporate office of Marriott (where we stayed) and commended the staff on the exceptional service. I am still in contact with one of the staff to this day. She said it was really a big thing, and they all were grateful that I had done such a wonderful thing for them. I had such a satisfaction hearing that. The staff that I mentioned in my letter received awards! The Hotel staff all were great, as I have found with other hotels and extended stays that I have had. For these people to go above and beyond for your needs is awesome. You may think, that is their job. But, when the hotel is your home away from home, and probably more time is spent at the hotel, for them to make you feel at home is quite something.

Working out of town is not for everyone. It takes a strong constitution. It is hard being away from your home. And no one knows the mental and physical hardship of doing it, until they do it. It is very easy to say you can do it, but until you live it, you don't know. Imagine living in a hotel for weeks at a time. You have the weekends to catch up. To catch up on the yard work, the laundry, the groceries, the bills, the cleaning, the home maintenance, anything that needs to be done. You know how you feel when you have been on vacation? At the end of the vacation, you are ready to go home. To sleep in your own bed. To be in your own home. To be in your familiar surroundings. Try to imagine just a day or two living like this, then try to imagine being away for a longer period. There are some advantages though, of staying away from home for work, for instance, in most situations, you tend to not spend as much money during the week.

If you are home, you are free to do more, thus you are most likely to spend money. You may spend more money on entertainment, food, gas or any other activity that you would not be able to do if you were cooped up in a hotel after work hours. Another plus is hotel points. I try to make sure wherever I stay, I get points from the hotels reward program. Eventually, you can redeem those points for a free hotel stay.

On one occasion, after working on the Ohio project, I had enough points to stay at a hotel in

Hawaii for free. I saved at least 100,000 points, probably more not having to pay for lodging. All I had to pay for was air fare and everything else during the stay. Totally worth it, and it was a great vacation!

Here is a great story. My cousin Sarah, whom had gone with me on this great experience, decided to make a memory worth keeping. We had spent a day sight seeing and we were back in the room for the rest of the night. My cousin, who was not a person to just sit and be entertained, decided that we should feed the seagulls. We started to do this by throwing food for them from the balcony located as part of our room. Before too long, we had a great number of seagulls landing on our balcony looking for dinner which we were providing. But this was not sufficient enough for us. At some point, my cousin decided that we should get a picture, or a video of a seagull grabbing Doritos from her mouth! We did just that! I actually have a video of my cousin lying on the floor of the balcony with Doritos in her mouth until a seagull takes it from her mouth. We burst into laughter at the absolutely stupid act.

But what about the time spent out of town? I have to say that many great conversations have happened at a simple meeting place offered by a hotel. A place where on a sunny day, you can feel the sun on your skin, on a rainy day you can feel the moisture on your breathe, a place where you can be human. You meet people, especially when you are "hanging out." I have met a lot of great people just sitting out in the sunshine. I met a genuinely nice man, "Larry," an African American man from Louisiana. I had many great conversations with him. He told me how I needed to visit Northern Louisiana. I asked him about where Bonnie and Clyde were killed, (which was in Northern Louisiana). He knew right where the spot was located. This man was a great cook. On a couple occasions, he made us dinner, just because we happened to be hanging out at the grill area. He always asked if we needed a drink when he saw we were empty. This is a person I was happy to call a friend. I was very disappointed to hear he got re-assigned and left the state. I never looked at him as a man of color. I looked at him as a great human being!

There are also many stories that happen you do not witness and you just seem to hear about from other people present at the time. Some stories I would hear would make me wish I had been there. Others I heard, I am glad I was not! I heard that some people (fellow co-workers) were hanging out and there happened to be a fire extinguisher in a case, in the grilling area. There were propane grills available, so if you wanted to cook dinner, you could and the extinguisher was there in case of a fire. One person I worked with, decided to break the case open with the hammer located beside the case to break the glass, take the fire extinguisher out and throw it in the garbage that was right next to the case.

He then proceeded to take the hammer that came with the case and do who knows what with it. I talked to this individual later and he didn't remember doing any of it. He did not know what he did with the hammer either. He was drinking of course. Oh, the stupid thing's people do when drinking. Myself included. A fellow employee, whom I stayed with at the most recent hotel, seemed to like to drink liquor and whisky from a measuring cup. Maybe so he knew the exact amount he was ingesting, so that he did not exceed his limit. I seriously doubt that was the reason because I saw him plenty of times WAY over the limit for anyone!

This co-worker told me that he and an ex-employee, (the same one who stole the fire extinguisher) used to hang out every night and get very intoxicated. I saw them one of the nights. And YES, they were intoxicated! These guys were in there 30's, and partied till 11 pm or later, but they still managed to get to work at 6 or 6:30 am every day, so there should be no excuse for not being on time for anyone else! This co-worker told me that they spent a lot of time in one of their hotel rooms and from time to time got rowdy, doing who knows what and would cause damage to the room.

I visited the room on one occasion and the door to a closet was ripped right off the hinges. Now, I should mention that these guys were in the same room every week and have the room cleaned upon request, so you can go for some time without housekeeping entering the room. They had to have used this to their advantage, because they would repair the room when it was damaged and then go on to live life like a normal human being. So they fixed the broken door and put it back on the hinges before the hotel found out. I also was told the same adult children put holes in the hotel room walls. Once again, I have no idea what the hell they were doing. Maybe they were wrestling or something, but the co-worker who is no longer with the company, told me they peeled paint off the walls in the room so they could go to the fix-it store and get materials and match the paint to repair the holes. So, as it turns out, the hotel remodeled, and it didn't even know it. I do not think they know it to this day.

One time I ran into a guy one time outside the hotel that seemed to be acting a bit weird. He overheard a phone conversation I was having and proceeded to interject his perception of the conversation. I just brushed him off as being drunk. I ignored him and finished my phone call as he continued his journey walking the perimeter of the hotel. About an hour later, I myself was going for a walk around the hotel, when I came to a grilling area, where angry groups of people were congregating. I apparently had just missed an altercation. They proceeded to tell me some guy that seemed to be "on something" was picking fights and disrespecting women. As I was getting the story, the same guy I encountered earlier showed back up in the heat of things for a second round. As people were getting ready to do battle, myself and another "levelheaded" gentleman, stepped in and told the unwanted guest, that he should just go to his room and not come back. He left and I never saw him again. I guess the hotel should have been paying me to do security. Although on many occasions, I was instigator of problems.

There was an occasion, where a couple of co-workers and myself had been tossing back a few. These guys were talking about going down to the front desk and fraternizing, with the help. But they seemed to not have the courage to do it. Me being the instigator, I talked them into doing it. I do not know what was more fun, watching the girls at the front desk, giving the guys a hard time, or watching the guys act drunkenly stupid towards the women!

I went down later and apologized for bringing them down, but I was assured that it was all in good fun! Things like that make the night of the hotel staff! I guess it makes the hotel staff's job less boring! While staying at the current hotel at this writing, I have found the staff to be more than just "people checking you in." They have gone above and beyond what you would expect from a regular place to stay. For instance, I spoke with a gentleman that has stayed at the hotel for a year such as myself, but unlike me, he has a dog that he brings with him every week. He said that he sometimes would work a twelve-hour shift. So the dog is in the room for twelve hours. Members of the staff take it upon themselves to go into his room, with permission of course, and take the dog out for a walk for exercise and to use the bathroom. I have never heard of that in my life! The sales manager Elena and another woman named Selena that works the front desk, always make sure that I am taken care of during my stay. As do all of the staff. I consider a couple of the staff that I have got to know while staying there a friend, especially Elena. I hope they consider me the same and not just a guest.

Just recently, near where I'm staying at this writing, I encountered a man and woman pan handling. The woman never really talked, it was always the man. They were probably in there early thirties. I had just walked out of the gas station close to this hotel and the man accosted me. He said, "Sir, do you think you could spare some change, we are looking to get a hotel room, but don't have quite enough. I replied, "I collect coins, so I really don't want to give anything up until I have checked them out. I actually do collect coins, so I was not just saying that. He responded, "I have a 1942 penny". I said, "Well I would trade a quarter for that." I had looked through my change and found a quarter I knew was not worth anything. He happily made the trade. He asked, "What do you think the penny is worth"? I told him, "Probably ten to thirty cents depending on the condition of it." We parted ways and I hurriedly made my way back to the hotel room to check out what I just received. I found that the 1942-penny was probably worth about fifteen cents in its condition. So I find myself walking up to the same gas station about a week later and meet the same two people on the sidewalk along the way. The guy gives the hotel sob story again. I said, "You asked me the same thing last week." "You gave me your

1942 penny." He said, "Oh ya, did you look that up? How much was it worth?" I told him, "About fifteen cents to twenty-five cents." He said, "Oh that's cool," and they continued on along the sidewalk.

After I made my purchase at the gas station, I walk out and headed back to the hotel. These same two people were right outside the gas station door asking people for money. They didn't ask me anything this time. I guess they remembered me from fifteen minutes prior! While out here working out of town, I at some point ran over a screw. It made the tire have a slow leak. One thing you don't want while living out of town are car problems. I tried to put a plug in it at the hotel while the tire was on the car. I have had luck previously doing this on other vehicles, but this time it was not working because it was in a tough spot, it didn't work. It was still leaking. I decided I needed to jack up the car and pull the tire off and plug it.

So I pulled around to the back of the hotel and I found a co-worker in back of the hotel having a cigarette. I told him my problem and he said, "I will call the mechanic here and he will help you." Before I knew it, the mechanic "Joel" came out, started his work truck and had my car jacked up.

He pulled the tire off my car and I plugged the hole. He put the tire back on the car and it was done. He saved me so much time and frustration. I tried to offer him some sort of compensation, but he would not take it. He said, "I just like to help people." This is what the world needs. More people like this gentleman. He finally accepted that he would receive some oatmeal raisin cookies and maybe a gift card to a restaurant he liked. I truly love meeting people like this out here while on "the road." I think it makes me want to be a better person. Just a little bit!

CHAPTER 12
JUST LUCK

Luck is something everyone wishes they had. Superstitious people do weird things to bring about good luck. Do not walk under a ladder, don't walk in front of a black cat, throw salt over your shoulder and the list goes on and on. I have watched people playing a slot machine at a casino and touch the screens in a certain order in the hopes that they will hit a jackpot. And have you ever been to bingo? People set out little trolls and all sorts of goofy things in the hopes that they will win. But what exactly are people looking for? Is it wealth, maybe good health or just a good life? Luck may come unexpectedly when you need it. You may not wish for it, but it may happen.

What strikes me as amazing are the stories that my Grandfather told us throughout the years before he passed away. I wish to this day that I had recorded the conversations, so I could write them down as they were spoken exactly. I would sit in awe, visualizing in my head what was being told to me. And I cannot imagine what he went through.

My Grandfather served in World War 2 and was captured by the German opposition about a year into the war. He told us how they marched him across Europe. I cannot imagine the fear of being shot at any given moment. The smell of gunpowder and the fog of war always are burning your eyes at every moment. He spoke of how at the prisoner camp, he ate burnt toast, and did not complain, because that is all there was to eat. How the German officers at Christmas would laugh and say, "Nein, no, you are nut going home, you vill stay here und rebuild Germany!" How one morning German soldier came into the prisoner barracks and yelled, "ROUST" (which means get up). And when my Grandfather did not move fast enough, the German solder hit him in the jaw with the butt of his rifle. By the way, he had hearing problems for the rest of his life after that. I am not sure if he received any compensation for that or not, but he should have.

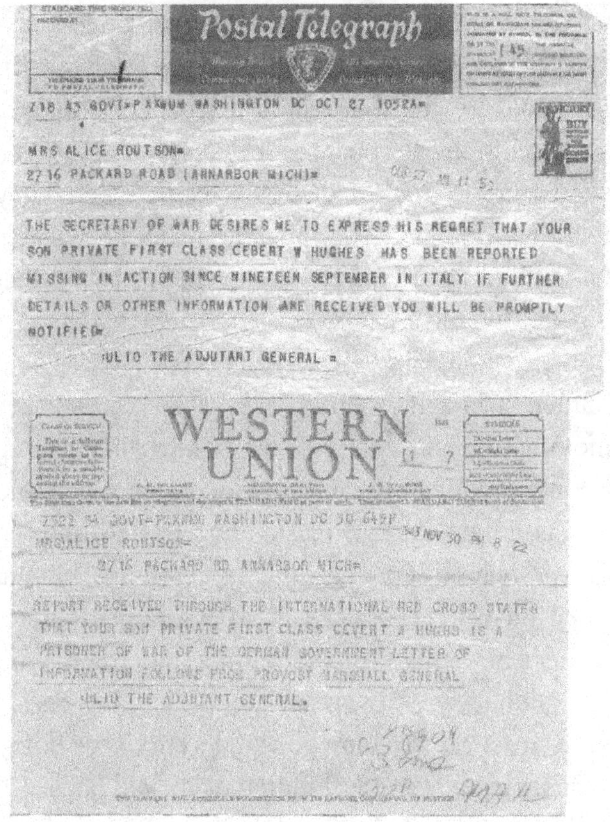

After my Grandfather was liberated from the camp in 1943, he was on his way on a lonely road, riding in a Truck with some Red Cross female volunteers and a fellow POW who had been freed, and were traveling together. After a long drive, they decided to stop for a rest.

My Grandfather got out and walked out to a nearby tree and stood and breathed in the fresh air. Listened to the birds chirping. The branches swaying in the cool breeze. The rest of the caravan stayed in the truck and stretched their legs. They felt as free as the air they breathed. My Grandfather started to hear a sound. A sound that got louder and louder. Started to get louder than the birds chirping. The sound got louder and louder, a buzzing sound. Like a swarm of bees moving ever closer. It was a humming like sound. Soon he realized it sounded like an airplane. And it was an airplane! Still standing by the tree, he moved behind it, using it like a man-made shield. Then he watched in horror as a German fighter plane sent bullets down, hitting the truck with precision. After he was sure this plane, the device of destruction was long gone, he went to see if any of his friends were still hiding as he had been. He called out, "Hello," "Are you there?" He walked up to the back of the truck, with his heart beating fast, still calling out, "Hey," "Are you ok." He opened the door to the back of the truck, only to find everyone dead. Blood stained the inside of the truck like a balloon filled with red paint had popped. All the female volunteers were killed. His friend sitting in the front of the truck was shot. He felt so lucky because he had decided to go stand behind a tree. I wonder if this tree is still there today in Germany. It is a lucky tree!

My Grandfather was also a police officer. He always had plenty of stories of the people he dealt with daily throughout his career. One of the stories I remember is that of a couple brothers who ran a Flint area mob in the 1960's, the Irwin brothers. I have a picture of my Grandfather transporting one of the arrested brothers to jail. He spoke of a story where an unsavory character the police had picked up at one time, spilling about the brothers, and some of their crimes, obviously trying to gain some sort of leverage with the knowledge he had to lessen his offense and possibly gain immunity from prosecution.

Prior to his arrest, the Irwin brothers felt he was a "squealer." They felt he was talking to the police. So they invited him to a meeting for a robbery. Late at night, they were driving him out into a golf course, where the meeting with other gang members was to take place. The man started to feel a cold feeling run down his spine as they drove farther into the meeting area and it got darker and darker. The conversation in the car seemed to end, and it became incredibly quiet. All he seemed to hear was the rumbling of the engine of the car and the noise from the road as they drove deeper and deeper into the darkness.

He started to feel like his life was about to come to an end. He opened the door and jumped out of the moving car. And then he ran. He ran for his life! As the car screeched to a halt, he bolted into the woods. "Come on, where are you going?" the voice broke into the night. "What are you doing" a different voice yelled out. "There is nothing to be afraid of, come back." But he kept running. He kept running it seemed until he was about to just drop. This man had possibly just escaped the jaws of death, and possibly an extremely torturous death. Anyway, when he was picked up later. It was his testimony, that the law used to catch the Irwin brothers and put them in prison. I am sure the man who testified felt lucky to be alive. Luck sometimes comes when you least expect it!

You may think my Grandfather was not incredibly lucky in life, because of being a prisoner of war. Spending a few years in a concentration camp and being brutalized by his German captors. So where is the luck in that, you may ask? While there is certainly not any luck in anything, he endured during World War Two, he certainly seemed lucky to us in his later years. My Grandfather did very well boxing in 1938. Before he went into the war in Europe, he had a phenomenally successful career as a boxer. He even won the Michigan Golden glove award in 1938. After my Grandfather got back from the war, he became a police officer. He even was a detective on the Michigan Murders or the killing of co-eds by John Collins, who was found to be the serial killer in the Ypsilant, MI. murders.

My maternal Grandfather also co-owned a successful racehorse named "Buzzby." A very busy man throughout his life was my Grandfather! But most of all, the family remembers him as being incredibly lucky at gambling. My Grandfather would seem to always win when he went to the casino. I am not talking about huge jackpot wins, but he seemed to win a thousand here or two thousand there. He once showed me some W2 tax forms for winnings. Two forms, one for $2000.00 and one for $4000.00, Not too bad of a win for one year. When the Michigan lottery game "Fantasy Five" came out, my Grandfather played it and won $100,000, he graciously gave all his children (which there are three) $5000.00 each out of the winnings. While my Grandfather was considered by us to be the lucky one, it was both my Grandfather and my grandmother that tried to share their good fortune to the family by giving wonderful Christmas gifts.

As far back as I can remember, we always got great gifts from them. One year I got a package of "Old Wisconsin Beef Sticks" I thought that was wonderful, because I just loved them! They gave us gifts like deodorant or soap, with the explanation, "You should always be clean and smell good!" There were gag gifts because my Grandfather loved jokes. Fake vomit or fake dog doo, whoopee cushions, you name it, we got it. As my Grandparents got older and we did, they were especially generous and began to give everyone cash gifts on top of the regular gifts. Then in the last few years, when my Grandfather was the only one of the two grandparents alive, he gave only cash gifts. And the gifts were generous beyond what a person could imagine. My Grandparents were, I think generous all through life, right up until it was the end. Maybe that is why, even though they both led a rough life in the beginning, towards the end, they may have been considered lucky.

CHAPTER 13
PASSING TIME

There must be some down time. A time when you are not in the hustle and bustle of the city, going to work or running from here to there. This is the time of relaxation. Not necessarily a vacation, but a vacation from the normal life. This is the time when you work on hobbies, read your favorite book or binge watch a television show. Something that helps you unwind from the normal every day chaos.

One of my favorite things I like to do is feed the birds. It doesn't matter if I'm at home or on vacation. I am in charge at home, to fill bird feeders. If the birds were depending on my wife Anna to feed them, they would probably starve to death! One of the first things I do when I get home from being out of town is put some birdseed in the empty feeders. My sister Laurel recently commented how surprised she was to hear that I know my bird types and am the general one in charge of the feeding. I guess growing up, I seemed gruff and course. I guess I still am. I do not think it takes anything away from a guy to want to feed these wonderful little creatures. I enjoy having them around the house. I have found that the Chickadees are very brave. Sometimes when they see me coming to fill the feeder, they will sit awfully close to the feeder, perhaps to be the first one at the food!

All of the other birds are scared and will fly away. I talk to the chickadees and say, "Hang on, I'm filling the feeder as fast as I can." Sometimes after I fill the feeder, I will stand there very still. It takes a few minutes, but the Chickadees will fly down to the feeder with me standing right next to it and get their food. They usually do not stay too long, because they don't quite trust the "large deliverer of food," but it's still cool. I remember one time I visited my Paternal grandmother up North in Michigan, she told me to take food down to her feeder and fill it. But before I put any feed in the feeder, put some in my hand, hold my hand out, and then stay very still. I did this, and eventually a chickadee landed in my hand and grabbed a mouthful of food, then flew off into a nearby tree. I thought it was so neat!

From time to time, birds will fly into our garage, and just can't seem to figure out that they simply need to fly back down under the garage door (we have a large door that opens with a remote) and then out of the garage, the way they flew in. But instead, they fly right up at the ceiling, bouncing off it like a rubber ball. Almost all the time that this happens, I must go out and sort of guide them out. This procedure usually takes quite a few minutes.

On one occasion, a hummingbird flew in and was having this same problem getting out of the garage. I tried for what seemed an hour to try to persuade the hummingbird out through the garage door. Using my hands, or a broom (do not worry, never actually touching the scared animal) to try to steer the poor hummingbird out to freedom.

Finally, after quite a long time, the bird lost all it's energy and finally landed on the cement floor of the garage. It is long pointed beak that you would usually see in a flower, or in a hummingbird feeder, was now wide open, in the shape of a "V." I had never seen this before. It had to have been, because it was dehydrated, and probably awfully close to death. I picked up the small hummingbird, and held it in my hand. Try and picture it. This little, exhausted, scared bird in the palm of my hand. It was quite a great feeling being able to help this wonderful animal.

I walked out to the front of my home where hummingbird feeder is located and placed him on one of the perches. My thought was he would immediately start drinking the sweet nectar. But to my surprise, he immediately flew from the feeder out to a nearby tree. I guess he had a little energy saved up yet! I do not know if he made it back to the feeder or not, but that was an incident I probably will never forget. Just something that not everyone gets to do in their life. Hold a hummingbird in their hand. Once, a Beautiful Cardinal flew into the front window of our home. We cannot figure out why this happens, since our windows tend not to be the cleanest!

The Cardinal was stunned from hitting the window, so I went outside and picked it up and put it up in a bush, I am fearful that if I leave the bird where it landed, a cat or other predator may come and eat it. So, I like to put the bird up high in a bush or tree until it recovers. On this occasion, we took a picture of me holding the Cardinal. It was clinging to my finger as a perch. I must admit, as much as I may dislike people, and the world in general, I really do like wildlife. Animals cannot make the decisions that humans do and thus they cannot be held responsible. I must say that it is quite something to hold a helpless animal in your hand and help it. To me, that is the best thing you can do in life!

A funny story about just "passing the time" is not one told by me, but it is a memory of my Father's. When my Father was in the Air Force, one of the duties he had was guarding the aircraft on the base. They worked in shifts of two and walked around the perimeter of the area to make sure that no one unauthorized was in the area. After weeks of this boring task, my Father and his fellow patrolman decided to make a "game" out of the task. While patrolling, they would try and sneak up on each other to see if they could catch each other off guard and sort of in Ninja like style prove that the other person was not doing a very good job.

One night my Father was on patrol, he was trying to stay more in the shadows of the aircraft, which was cast by the moonlight in the sky. He was very stealthy that night. He became part of the shadow. He noticed a figure up by the hanger of an aircraft. This person was walking away from my father and had not seen him. My father thought, "Oh, I'm gonna get him good," as he started creeping slowly in the direction of the person walking along the outside of the hanger. As he got about 20' from the figure, my Father yelled out "Halt, who goes there." My father, feeling absolute satisfaction that he had just caught his patrol mate off guard and had won the game, stood there waiting for his patrol cohort to turn and say, "You got me." The person turned in surprise to meet the voice bellowing from behind him and it was my fathers Lieutenant from the squad. My Father stood silent not knowing what to say. He had been caught playing this game! The Lieutenant said, "Good job, I didn't even hear you come up to me." The Lieutenant walked away with the sense that things were under control for the night. My father felt like he had gotten rewarded for playing a game. Not too shabby!

CHAPTER 14
FLIPPING OUT

Around the year 1990, it became a big thing to rehab or "flip" houses. To those of you who don't know what this is and have not watched the many shows on television where people do this, it's when people buy a house, usually a home that is in need of repair. A "fixer upper." They go through the house and remodel it to new quality. Usually, the amount they put into the house paid off. There were many reality television shows about it. People making huge amounts of money doing it. There are many shows on television today that still do it. As a matter of fact, while vacationing in Hawaii, I met the stars of the original "Flip This House." I had a nice conversation with the realtor of the show while relaxing in the hotel hot tub. She was a very nice woman. She was not one of those people that let the stardom go to her head. To be honest, I didn't remember her right away. She introduced herself and mentioned she was in the show and that they were there to look at Hawaii properties to flip.

In 2003, my brother Kent and I decided to try our hand at starting our own business flipping houses. We scraped some money together a bought our first home to remodel. It was more than we expected as you may have guessed. It was in the wonderful city of Albion, Michigan. The home was located in a residential area of the city and was probably a moderate crime area. Shortly after we bought the place, someone stole a fountain that was in the front yard. It was probably the neighbor. We started to rehab the home and we had our share of "stupid" moments.

For instance, we were carpeting the downstairs and I was cutting the carpet to fit against the wall and proceeded to cut the under side of my arm with the utility knife. I think I had nicked a vein. It bled well for a while, but I managed not to get any blood on any of the new carpets. I did a wrap of the wound, but it kept bleeding and drenching the towel. Yes, I was using shop towels as my bandage, and wrapping it with duct tape, because that was all that was handy. I kept redressing the wound, and probably went through a roll of shop towels, before the bleeding slowed, and then finally stopped. That was dumb of me. But we have another "winner" of a time, that both my brother and I am guilty of.

We noticed a water leak one day, a slow leak, but a leak that certainly would not pass inspection at the time of sale. We spent all week, taking turns putting in a coupling and sealing it, and then coming back, probably driving 30-45 minutes to check on it. We did these four or five times, and then we bought a compression coupling and BOOM, the water leak was solved. Both of us felt quite stupid about this. I guess it was a learning situation. We worked on the home for about three months, and after a few months on the market and a change of realtors, the home sold, and we had made a very nice profit. My brother Kent and I decided to take the money and invest it in another property. But this time, we would buy a home closer to home, in the city of Jackson, Michigan.

After buying the property, we talked to some of the neighbors and they said they thought that the house used to be a "crack house." With this new wonderful information, we started work on the home. We had met the neighbor across the street and talked to him a few times, and he had proclaimed that his job was catering. He said, "I do breakfast," "Breakfast is my job."

My brother Kent, one day after work was on his way to the work house and had seen this neighbor and for some reason, unknown to me, picked him up and gave him a ride to his house across the street from our work house. I guess Kent is some great humanitarian. So, along the way, this neighbor starts talking about how he is a great boxer and starts punching the windshield. Kent said to him, "If you keep boxing my windshield, I'm gonna box your head." The guy immediately stopped hitting the windshield. That was pretty much the last time we heard from that neighbor.

On this house, we planned on spending a little more and making the inside of the house look good, even though the house was in a not so good neighborhood. We put up crown molding in the living room, we did up the dining room with nice wood trim halfway up the wall, and a nice chandelier for the light. Anything to help us sell the house. But if we thought the remodeling of this home contained no stupid actions, we were mistaken. The ceiling in the living room was in very bad shape, so we decided to just drywall the whole living room ceiling put up the drywall mud on all of the seams, sand the seams, then paint the whole ceiling. It looked so good after it was finished! We then moved to the upstairs of the house to remodel the rooms (as it was a two-story house). I started to pull up the carpet in the room directly above the living room. The old carpet pulled up so easily. I had started from the doorway and started moving into the room. About halfway into the room, I stepped into a heating vent in the middle of the room. My foot went to the bottom of the vent, through the vent, and through the ceiling of the living room. A brand-new ceiling! I felt so stupid, and Kent told me I was so. We moved back to the living room and worked on fixing the damage I had done. We used drywall screws to put the ceiling back up, where it was hanging down. We re-mudded the area that needed mudding. Kent was handling the mudding of the ceiling on this one. He did probably one of the best covering jobs he had ever done. There would not have to be much sanding on the ceiling, because of Client's masterpiece of mudding job.

After he was finished, he started down the ladder that was set up for fixing the ceiling. He was still looking at his Michael Angelo piece of work ironically on the ceiling when he stepped into a five-gallon bucket of drywall mud. I laughed at his stupidity. Finally, I was not the only Idiot working here! Our last attempt at this business was still a home in Jackson, Michigan. We got the home for a good price, but it was right next to a store, so in hindsight, it probably was not a good investment. This house was once again, not in a good area. The first evidence of this was, I had made the mistake of leaving a push lawn mower at the residence for lawn care. I returned the next day to find that the gas had been drained from the lawn mower. After we remodeled the house, it stood for sale, for a summer and a winter. I always seemed to go over about once a week to check on the premises. Make sure that everything was ok.

During the winter, I stopped over and walked up to the door and for some reason, I didn't use my key, I just turned the knob. And it opened. That was a major red flag! I walked into the house and noticed it was very hot. I walked to the living room where the thermostat was at and it was set to 80 degrees. Normally we left it at about 60 degrees. I then looked to the front door, which had a top pane that had been replaced with a piece of Plexiglas, but it had simply been pushed or knocked inwards and then the front door was unlocked, opened and an intruder had entered and made themselves at home. They had cranked the heat up, because it was winter to make their stay more comfortable and had left the side door unlocked to make re-entry easier. I had the police come out. A black officer arrived and looked around and said they would watch the house for us. I don't think they did anything, but luckily there were no more break-ins that winter. I continued to go over to the home about once a week for the winter and into spring and onto the summer.

One summer day, I entered the home one Sunday morning and as soon as I entered the side door, there was a coat lying on the floor. I was thinking, "This shouldn't be here." A coat lying on the floor. Like someone had walked in the door and dropped their coat on the floor. I went into the downstairs bathroom and found a bottle of shampoo sitting on the sill of the shower. Now this home was supposed to be vacant, uninhabited. Why was there a shampoo bottle? I thought, maybe Kent had needed to stay at the house, and that is why I was finding these things. I crept up the stairs that led to the upper level of the house. It was about 8:00 am, Sunday morning, I'm standing at the top of the stairs, and walk into the room at the top of the stairs and what is it I see? There is a boy, about ten to twelve years old, lying on the floor, fast asleep. I started to kick him gently in the back, not really thinking that he could have been armed with a gun. He muttered in a sleepy voice, "Do you know who I am?" I said, "I don't care, wake up." After waking the boy up, I said, "What are you doing here? this is a private residence." He replied, "The door was open." "No, it wasn't," I said. After a few minutes of going back and forth, I said, "Look, you are in a private home." "Let's call the police." He said, "Please don't." I said, "Ok, I am going to do something I hope you remember; I'm going to let you go." "Tell your friends this place is off limits." The kid started to head towards the window in the room. That is probably how he got in. I watched him put up the window, open the screen and proceed to go through the window onto the roof, shut the screen and close the window. He then jumped down from the roof onto the ground from about 10 to 12 feet up. As he hit the ground I heard him say, "Ouch". It was a minimal punishment as far as I was concerned. I never found anyone else in the home after that.

Being your own boss is quite fulfilling. It is a lot of work and you get a great amount of satisfaction from it. If I were able to do it, I would like to be flipping houses still to this day. Here is a word of warning. NEVER rent to some one. They are renting for a reason. They have bad credit. They don't pay their bills. Do you want to be the person to deal with someone irresponsible? Never pays on time, if they pay at all? We got tired of it. We got rid our last home and stopped flipping. We have never looked back!

CHAPTER 15
THE LAW

I am sure at some point everyone has had some sort of brush with the law. It is most likely speeding, which is probably the most violated law. It also may be drunk driving, which is also probably the next most violated law. Some people can tell you of their exploits in the county lock up or the state prison system. Neither being in county Jail or the State or Federal prison system should be a bragging point, although some people think they are. A perceived "normal" life should not contain any of these.

I have had my fair share of minor brushes with the law. A few speeding tickets, a couple of accidents, and a couple of minor infractions. Three of which were in a company truck. Two of them were for doing about 40-45 in a 25 mile per hour zone, and the third, I was doing 70 miles per hour in a 45 miles per hour construction zone. But the construction zone ticket was a funny one. It was only 45 if they had flashing lights going. Neither the co-worker I was with nor myself noticed construction lights flashing, but the officer said they were, so of course I got the ticket. And it was $240.00.

One of the accidents I got into, I had just turned 18 years old and was going to pick up a birthday present from the store. Leather jacket. On the way to the store, I ran into some traffic on the highway. It was stop and go. I noticed a police officer a few cars ahead, which may have been an accident, I do not remember. The car in front of me started to move, so I gently pressed on the gas and proceeded forward with the rest of the traffic. I think for whatever reason I looked out the driver's window, or maybe glanced at the door mirror, at the rest of the cars backed up for at least a mile behind me. When I looked back ahead to the car in front of me, it had its brakes on. Yes, brake lights were lit up red! I jammed on the brakes, but still ran into the back of the car in front of me.

Luckily, we were not going that fast, so there really wasn't any damage done to either vehicle. There was a Police officer on the road a few cars up from mine. He walked up to my car window, which was already down, because it was warm out. Yes, a nice birthday, nice weather, going to pick up a present and what does the Officer say when he reaches my window? Not "Are you ok?", He said, "I'm giving you a ticket." I did not know what to say, so I replied in a loud and belligerent voice, "OK." It was not my finest moment. I would wear leather jackets for many years. I would be known for wearing them. I recently went into the local bank, where I saw a woman that I went to school with, that works at the bank, and helped me with my banking needs, also remarked, "I see you are still wearing leather jackets, just like you did in high school." I wore leather jackets in high school all the time. I wore them most of my adult life.

Another brush that I had with the police I'm fond of I like to talk about is the time I got pulled over in my Trans Am. I had just left a friend's house, which had bought a six-pack of beer for me. It was a humid Michigan day and beer seemed to help with the heat that day. You see currently; I was not of legal age to buy alcohol. I had two drinks out of it and left to go into town to drive around in my muscle car. Yak, I agree, stupid. I do not remember why I was pulled over for sure, but

I knew I was in trouble. The Officer noticed the beers sitting in the back seat that I had proudly on display, apparently. He had me get out of my car and placed me in handcuffs. He asked me, "When did you get the beer"? I responded, "Oh, I have had thoughts for a while." He said back with disbelief, "Well, they are sweating from the heat and looking pretty desirable." I think we will search your car. They put me in the back of the squad car. I remember it being so hot in the car. The engine was not running, so there was no air conditioning, and they had a baseball game playing on the car radio. Probably WJR radio. So I was sitting in the back seat of the hot police car, listening to the baseball game on the radio, as I watched them search my Trans Am and place what they found on the top of the car. A half empty, or half full fifth of Peach Schnapps. Yes, I forgot that it was on the back floor from a previous party. A radar detector that I had bought from someone in school, that supposedly had stolen it from a store. And a genuinely nice ivory handle switch blade. I do not remember where I got it, or why I had it, but for some reason I had put it in the center console and forgot it was there. I listened to the police CB as they ran the serial number of the radar detector.

After a few minutes, the dispatcher came back on the air waves with the words, "That Item comes back clean." I breathed a sigh of relief, even though I was still sitting in the back seat of a police car in hand cuffs. I thought my goose was cooked, I thought for sure I was going to jail. I was afraid they were going to ask me who bought me the alcohol, since I was a minor. The officer came and opened the back door to the police car and had me get out. He said in a low growling voice, "I could take you in for carrying a concealed weapon, and minor in possession, but I am willing to let you off with just a ticket for having an open intoxicant."

Yes, I forgot to mention I had an open beer I was sipping out of when I was pulled over, that I threw on the floor, so on top of everything, there was a beer smell in the car. I said in a high voice, "Sounds fair to me." So, he unlocked the handcuffs, that were causing my wrist to go numb, and wrote me the ticket for an open intoxicant. As he handed me the ticket, he said, "Oh, you can try to fight for your illegal switchblade, which is considered a concealed weapon, in court, and possibly go to jail for having it, or you can just let me confiscate it." I said without a second thought, "It's yours."

As a last sort of lesson, the Officer had me pour out the remaining beers on the side of the road. His partner laughed as he said, "Some dog may get drunk tonight!" As I drove away from this scene, I felt the world lift off my chest. And I later relayed the story to friends that night. But the story does not end here, unfortunately. I still had to go to court about the ticket. I have always been a person that believes in handling my business and problems myself. So I got all dressed up in nice clothes, I didn't tell anyone what I was doing and went to court in front of the Magistrate, to face the music. I had to deal with the ticket. I had never been in a courtroom before, so I was full of fear. I just sat and waited as the Magistrate went through the morning cases.

Right before I was called, a guy was called for the exact same thing I was there for. This guy was not really dressed up at all, in fact his shirt had a rip in the front, and he looked like a bum. The Magistrate read the bums crime, "First offense open intoxicant, how do you plead?" The disheveled guy said, "No contest." The Magistrate looked at this not so well dressed man and said, "$100.00 fine." "Next on the docket, Chad Young, charged with open intoxicant, first offense". I stood very slowly from my seat and said in a low mouse like voice, "No contest your Honor." He responded very quickly, like he already had it planned out, "$50.00 fine." I felt fairly good. I even thought maybe me dressing up may have helped me get a lower fine, since the guy before got a $100.00 dollar fine for the same thing! So, this was my first time and the last time in court for an infraction! I said that I did not go into Court again in my life. I did not say it was my last brush with a law Officer. But this last one is the best of all.

Back in my younger years, I had a few muscle cars. I had a 69' Ford Mustang, a 72' Dodge Charger, a 78' Trans Am, an 85' Ford Mustang, an 87' Ford Mustang and I currently have a 2008 Shelby Mustang. I have to say, that the Mustangs were the most powerful. The Shelby Mustang is at the top of the list.

During the time I was 17 or 18, I had the 72' Dodge Charger, I happened to work with a guy that had an Impala. Maybe it was a 1970 Chevy Impala. He had done a few things to the motor, to "soup" it up and make it faster, so he was talking one night after work. At this time, we both worked at the Methodist Home in Chelsea MI. He was saying how fast his car was, and how it would leave mine in the dust. Me, being the type that did not really care who had the faster car, said, "Maybe we should race them out on Industrial Dr." Industrial Dr was just a large "U" shaped road that wrapped around a few businesses just on the outskirts of Chelsea, MI. It is still there today. It is probably not even a quarter of a mile on the straight parts of the road, but it was enough to win a race!

So we decided to find out who had the faster car. He drove off in his Impala to the race spot, and I took off in my 72' Dodge Charger with another friend from work. The same friend who lit off the M-80 out of my 69' Mustang when I owned that. Yes, we were both bad influences on each other. So, we speeded out to the race site on Industrial Dr. we lined up the cars by their front ends. We both had our windows down and one of us counted down, "3, 2, 1, GO". We both floored our vehicles. I do not even remember who won the race. Maybe it was so close, we decided to go again. We drove down the road and pulled into the "U" shaped Industrial Dr. again. As we pulled around to the straight part of the road, a local police car that I had not noticed pulled in behind me and turned his lights on. I pulled over, and the other hot rodder in the Impala slowly kept going, probably hoping to make a clean getaway.

The Policeman pulled along side my car and said in a threatening voice, "Stay here, don't you move." And he sped off to catch the Driver in the Impala, who was trying to make a clean break. The police officer turned on his flashing lights behind the Impala, which was now pretty far down the road by this time. The officer then instructed him to go back into the Industrial Dr, Back to where I was parked, and that he park on the opposite side of the road, across from me. So after the driver of the Impala got back to where I was, the Impala's driver door was across from my driver's door. The police car pulled in behind my car and the officer got out and walked up to the car. And this is the first time I realized who the Police Officer was. He was the older brother of a friend of mine throughout the school.

Now I didn't know "Buddy" very well, but I knew who he was and he knew me. He was a complete professional. He did not act for a second like he knew me. He stated, "This is very dangerous to be doing this." And "Someone could very easily get hurt." I gave him my registration and insurance, which he asked for. Then he walked over towards the guy in the Impala. At this point, for some reason, I got very cocky. I turned on the radio. Played some rock music. Not real loud, but loud enough that you could hear it. The music seemed loud, but we still could hear the officer interacting with the driver in the Impala. We could hear the Impala driver beg the police officer, "Please don't give me a ticket!" Both my friend and I laughed in my car at the other driver being a baby. Eventually, "Buddy" came back to my car after spending some time in his squad car and said, "I'm going to let you off with a warning, but I don't want to see this car in town the rest of the night, or you will get a ticket." I said, "That's no problem at all. Thank you, Officer."

The Police car left us in his dust, and we were left all alone. The three of us all sat there, processing what had just transpired. The Impala driver came over and said, "What's the matter with you guy's?" "What do you mean?" I said with a loathing tone to my voice. He said, "You guys seemed like you were just trying to get busted, I heard you laughing, and playing the radio." He was not incredibly happy. So, we left the area. I dropped my passenger off and took my Charger home to my Parents house, where I lived at the time. And in a sort of defiance, I made up a story to my parents and borrowed their car and took it back into town to my friend's house, that had just been riding with me in the Charger. We got a good laugh, as I told the story AGAIN, that he had already told the fellow friends that were there. Ah, the stupid things we do as kids. But at least I always took responsibility for my actions and paid the price if necessary. Luckily, this was one of the times where it pays to know someone!

CHAPTER 16
HARD TIMES

What is the definition of "hard times"? Is it having your house demolished by a tornado? Is it your parents are killed in a plane crash? Is it you have a miscarriage? Is it your car is destroyed by hail? Is it you are a captured solder? There can be many definitions of this question. It really depends on the individual. It depends on what the individual can handle and what they consider as hard that pertains to their life. Hard can only be perceived as no longer one can be able to handle it.

In 2011, I lost my job that I had for 11 years due to the economic downslide. It was very devastating. And I still have not completely recovered from it. No one can know what you feel unless they experience it. It really took a month before it really began to sink in. I really didn't worry about paying bills when it happened because

I had a small amount saved up. But as I watched it start to dwindle, reality began to be more obvious. Luckily, I instantly began cost cutting. I only bought things I deemed necessary. I was laid off during the winter, so I started dressing very warm and setting the heat at 57 degrees while I was home. I changed all of the light bulbs to 40-watt bulbs and I bought minimum food to live on. I ate Little Caesuras pizza religiously. A 5-dollar pizza would last 3 days. I also ate hot dogs quite a lot. That is what I remember eating the most often.

I was able to get unemployment, but that would only cover my house payment, the car and house insurance, the electric bill, a small amount of gas money to move about, propane for heating, and then you had what was left to buy a small amount of groceries to survive on. Luckily, I had my parents, who would have me over for dinner as often as I wanted for a full stomach. I lived like this for 6 months to almost a year. Yes, it was that hard to get another job at the time! I kept a record of everywhere I applied during the time and it was about 110 businesses. Because of all of this, I am very conservative to this day and I have no empathy for people who are irresponsible with their money. LIVE WITHIN YOUR MEANS!

I worked many jobs I didn't like, including working out of town or even out of state, in order to keep my house and really continue to live. I didn't like being on unemployment. It felt demeaning. I tried to get food stamps. Yes, I felt I had hit an all time low by applying for this. But after filing, I was told by the state that I made too much and in the end, I was allowed 20.00 a month. Not even worth the time I spent applying.

Today looking back, I feel empowered, because I hit a low in life and was able to still make my house payment, never missing one payment and got back on my feet. Pride is a long lost thing nowadays.

Losing my job in 2011 was however anticipated. The people in my office could see the writing on the wall, so we knew it was coming. A group of us took the job of working in Ohio for what turned out to be about a year and a half. It started out with us having to drive our personal vehicles down to the job in Ohio. I had an older truck that had many miles on it and needed some work. I had about $1200.00 worth of suspension work done and drove down to Ohio 1 or two times. Then it was decided it would be cheaper to have us all ride down to Ohio in a company vehicle. I exclaimed to the Vice President of the company that made the decision, "I just put 1200.00 worth of work into my vehicle!" "I'm sorry" is what I got back from him.

So, we continued to ride down together in the company vehicle to Ohio for the next year and a half. Meeting at the office about 5 am, then leaving for Ohio and arriving about 7 am. There were 4 of us and we would take turns driving. I guess I should say two of us would take turns driving. There was another co-worker, Pete and myself. We were the drivers. The other passengers never had to drive. One was a project manager and he was on his laptop from the time we left, the other was a restricted driver because of accidents. This is how it went for the next year and a half. The restricted driver would sleep for the entire drive from the office in Michigan to the office to Ohio. One of the times while driving, I was tired of the restricted driver snoring during the ride. I drove over to the shoulder of the rumble strip so that it made a lot of noise and woke him up! While working in Ohio, we did manage to have a good time. We spent at least 1 night a week at a restaurant called the Blue Snapper. It had an outdoor patio with a bar and was a great area to relax.

One time we had to stay the weekend to get some work done and at the end of the day, Pete and myself decided to have dinner at the "Snapper" which is what we called it by this time. There happened to be a Bachelorette party going on, so we decided to "crash" it. I talked to the sisters of the bride for some time. They were very nice gals. I even have pictures of them to this day. I bought the wedding party a round of shots that cost 80.00, and according to Pete, I was hitting on the bride, although I don't remember doing that!

CHAPTER 17
PARTY TIME!

PARTY! Everyone knows the meaning. And everyone has his or her memories of parties they attended or threw. It may be a graduation, a wedding, or a simple gathering. The best part of it is you don't even need a reason. You can have a party all by yourself! Although this isn't suggested! There are many reasons for a party. A super bowl, a baby shower or even passing a test, the reasons are limitless. The main reason for a party is to remember it. And if you remember it, it was therefore memorable!

I have been to many parties! When I was in high school, and even to the present time. It's pretty much the same experience, with one exception. You act a certain way depending on your age level at the time. Or depending on some people I know, you act like a fool every time! In high school, yes, I was the person who may have acted like a fool. And even as a young adult, I still may have acted like a fool. But now that I am older, when I'm at a party, I'm just there socializing. I hope anyway!

In high school, when someone would announce a party. They would pick a when and a where. The time was never really given. I suppose it was just when it was starting to get dark. In my late teens, I remember a party I attended at Crooked Lake, which is near Chelsea, MI. There were many people in attendance. This was a great time. You would just mingle around. Some people you knew and would be like, "Hey, you're here?" Or you would meet people you didn't know and get into discussions, which were good since I was a freshman, I made a lot of friends. I could go to school the following week and be like, "Hey, what up?" And all of a sudden, I knew a lot more people in school.

At the Crooked Lake party, I hung out with a schoolmate and who now is my boss. Funny how some things work. I had known him all through school. Always a good friend. At this party, I ran into at least one person who was a bit of a bully toward me. I felt somewhat scared when I ran into him. I think someone introduced me to him. We talked for a bit before he stumbled on to talk to someone else. I don't believe he ever bullied me again. There is sort of an unwritten rule. If you meet someone at a blowout party, you are friends from now on!

I spoke with a young man who was a bit of a hoodlum who I got along with in school (imagine that) and that he was drinking from a bottle of Johnny Walker whiskey. We started just calling him Johnny, even though his name was Ken. He didn't care. He seemed to enjoy being "branded." I remember somehow about this night among all of the people stumbling around, that we felt free. It was a good time. The next day I went with a friend back to the party site. We thought it was a good idea to go see if there were any returnable bottles left behind. We picked up quite a few. It's amazing how at a party such as this, people are not worried about taking back cans or bottles for the refund. We took what we recovered back to the nearest store and turned them in and split the funds. We were happy to find anything at all.

Of the many parties I attended as a young adult, I remember one specifically. I went with a co-worker who boasted that college parties were the best parties. I rode with him to some party he heard about on the campus of Eastern Michigan University. We arrived at an apartment filled with people. As we were walking in, some big, dumb guy stepped in front of us.

I later found out he was playing football for EMU. He said to us, "Hey, I don't know you. I'm not gonna let you in here." I could have got belligerent and started pushing and shoving at such a statement, but seeing that the guy was twice the size of me and towered over me at least a foot, I calmly stated, "You know, someone told me about this party here tonight. They also said I would be able to hang out with the intelligent and athletic students here at EMU", (which I had just made up on the spot!) "Now, do you really want me to go back to this person and tell them that I was not let in?" This big guy looked at me for a minute, with god knows what going through his mind. He then yelled, "Come on in!" I shook his hand and patted him on the back as I walked by this hulking man, probably narrowly escaping a certain beating. We mingled about. I don't even remember anything more than a lot of people crowded into an apartment. It really wasn't that great of a party.

A time I remember after partying somewhere, was getting home and trying to sleep part of the equation. I must have been very drunk this night. After eating a Big Mac meal from McDonalds, I headed home. I still lived at my parent's home at this time. I crept up to my bedroom, trying to make as little noise as possible. I somehow found my way to my bedroom, which at the time I shared with my brother, got into my bed, and went to sleep. I don't know how long I had been asleep, but soon I found myself in a wilderness. I awoke and found myself to be sleeping on a cot in the woods! I recognized it to be the woods behind my parent's house. I felt so at home and relaxed.

Funny, I didn't seem to wonder how I had got there. But a problem soon became apparent. I felt as though I had an upset stomach. I felt as though I may have to vomit. I thought to myself, "I can just lean over the cot I am laying on in the woods and just release whatever needs to come out". There would be nothing to clean up, since it is indeed the woods. So, I leaned over the edge of the cot and proceeded to vomit. It was at this exact moment that I woke up and realized I was not out in the woods. I was in my bedroom and I was leaning over the edge of my bed and vomiting on the floor.

I watched as the Big Mac and fries I had eaten earlier came back out and expelled onto the floor next to my bed. This woke my brother up, whom I shared a room with. He simply got up and left the room. He probably went downstairs and slept on the couch in the living room. I think I even waited until the next morning to clean it up because I was too tired at the time! GROSS!

A time I remember, I was at my friend's mother's home in the Clear Lake area. We were enjoying a few beers at his Mother's home. He was in his twenties and lived with his Mother. She had no problem sitting with us having a beer or two, as we doubled and tripled her as far as beer intake. We spoke about things going on at work and at the time, all three of us worked at the same place.

Now I have to state the layout of this home. There was the living room where we were sitting and the kitchen was right off of that. Then a hallway led off to the kitchen. Down this hall was a stairway immediately to the left off the kitchen that led down to the basement, then the bathroom which was the next left after the stairway to the basement and continuing down the hall were the bedrooms. After consuming many, many beers, I found myself with an overly full bladder. Having been at this home many times before and knowing exactly where the bathroom was, I excused myself from the conversation with a calm and cool "I will be right back."

I got up from my seat and walked through the kitchen with the swagger that only a person of my caliber could emit. I turned immediately left after the kitchen and found myself tumbling down some bare wooden stairs. I rolled end over end. Side to side. As I reached the bottom of the landing in the basement, I probably attempted at saying something clever like "opps." I walked back up the stairs to the hallway and was met by two horrified looking faces. My friend and his mom were standing there wondering if I was ok. I probably exclaimed with arms raised, "All good," as I continued to the bathroom, which was the original destination.

Both my friend and his mother were relieved that I was not hurt. I don't think I even had a bruise from the incident. We continued the rest of the visit like nothing happened. The next time I worked together with my friend who witnessed the "accident" said, "Man, you gave my mom a heart attack when you fell down the stairs." "I'm so very sorry about that." "I'm sorry" is a phrase I would find myself saying a lot in life!

I briefly lived in an upstairs apartment just outside of the city of Chelsea, MI. Probably halfway between Chelsea and Manchester, I made the mistake of having a roommate. You have to live and learn, I guess. I was neat and he was not. He would leave dishes sitting in the sink and I didn't.

One weekend, the roommate decided to throw a party. And this guy had many friends. This was a small, upstairs apartment. There was a long stairway that led upstairs to the apartment. And there was a small balcony area in front of the apartment to sit and relax or stand and look out at the woods behind the place. A very small apartment soon was filled with all sorts of people. The place was packed. I couldn't believe there were so many people there. We had our own parking area on the side of the apartment and the landlord lived below and had a separate driveway. Our driveway was full and there were cars parked down the side of the road and down the adjoining road.

Soon our telephone rang. I answered it. On the other end was the landlord. He stated somewhat angrily, "Yea, there is a vehicle parked in our driveway and I would like it moved." I said, "I will get it moved immediately." And hung up. I looked out the apartment window and saw a black van in the landlord's driveway. I yelled out to the crowd in the apartment, "Who owns a black van?" Someone said, "I do," I said, "Well, you have to move it. You are parked in the landlord's driveway." Everyone went OOOWWWWW. The van was quickly moved.

I walked outside, sensing that things were out of control, just in time to see someone. I knew riding down the apartment stairs, which was a flight of at least 20' if not more, in a cardboard box. I'm not sure where the box came from. I told the person. "That's enough! Don't do that anymore." I walked back inside the apartment, where it seemed like it was even more full than it was when I just previously left. I was starting to get mad. Things were getting really bad.

All of a sudden, someone grabbed me and said someone was at the door and wanted to talk with me. What now, I thought. I got to the door and there was the Landlord and his wife, both in their pajamas. The landlord was fuming. He was hardly able to keep his composure. He angrily said, "This place is not set up to handle this kind of traffic," he continued, "you need to shut this down and get these people the hell out of here." With that, him and his wife turned and walked past the people that were crowding on the balcony, and walked down the stairs. I walked into the apartment and said in a loud voice, "The party is over, the landlord is pissed and everyone has to leave. I was amazed at how fast the apartment emptied. It went from jam-packed to immediately empty in a matter of minutes, it seemed. Except for a few people that we allowed to stay.

After all of this was over, I decided to make some macaroni and cheese. I stepped away from the stove for a minute and while I was away, the pan boiled over and the steam caused the smoke alarm to go off. The telephone rang again. But on this time the roommate answered. "Hello," he said with a shaky voice. It was the landlord again. The landlord asked, "I just wanted to make sure the place wasn't on fire." "No," my roommate exclaimed. "Chad just don't know how to cook."

After a few seconds of small talk with the landlord and deciding he was calmed down, my roommate hung up the phone and we all looked at each other and decided this was enough partying for one night. Soon after that, the roommate moved out. I decided to stay at the apartment and live there by myself, living alone and paying the entire rent myself, which was like 480.00 a month. After a few weeks, the landlord and his wife invited me to dinner and I accepted. It was a little awkward, until the landlord said, "Man, it's been so quiet since the other guy left, I guess he was the problem!" I said, "Yes, I'm quiet and have quiet friends when I have them over." After that night, I had no problems with the landlord for the rest of my stay there at the apartment.

Recently, I found out I was at a party that I had forgotten I even attended. I went to my local bank and the teller who works there that I went to school with said, "Hey, I have been waiting for you to come in." She took a few seconds to scroll through pictures on her phone and showed me a picture of me, probably in high school or just out of high school at a party for another person. I didn't really know why I was there. Must have gone with a friend since I didn't know the person whom the party was for. It's funny sometimes the small world we live in. I don't remember being at the party and I don't remember the picture being taken, but it is still neat to see myself back then. Clad in my trademark leather jacket that I wore everywhere. The teller friend at the bank even remembered that I always wore leather jackets!

Of all the partying that I did in my youth, it was almost never at my parent's house when they were away. I think I had a total of two parties at my parent's house and I asked their permission for both parties when they were not home. The first was just a party that was really a gathering of co-workers. It was all just people I worked with in Dexter at a place called Colorbok. There really was nothing special about this, except for the fact that at the time, I had a Trans Am that was soaped up. So, I wanted to show it off. I was taking people for rides down the road to the pavement at the end of the road by our church. I would peel out and drive to the end of the paved area down from the church, turn around and bring the vehicle back to the house. One of the last rides, I remember a neighbor came out to the edge of his property and yelled as we went by "SLOW DOWN"! Apparently, I had been driving too fast up and down our road, although I didn't think I had been.

The second party was a party for my band at the time to play at. We set up the equipment in my parent's garage. There is footage of this party somewhere. We even invited my Aunt Lowene and Uncle Jeff who lived down the road. It was basically a pretty tame gathering. The band played. People drank. And I made sure my parent's house was not destroyed by the people attending the party, I think my parents would be proud that I made sure their home and property was treated with the respect that anyone would expect.

CHAPTER 18
NEARING THE END

At some point, a book needs to come to an end. Never having written a book before, how is this done? Writing about experiences can go on until the day you die. At some point, you have to pick a stopping point. I guess I can just say something like as follows:

At fifty one years old at the time of this writing, I see too many people that live possibly a great life, but at the end of it, they may lose their memory and not remember any of it. This is such a terrible thing. To have lived a life and not even remember it! There may be many adventures that happened throughout your life. I know of many people that have traveled and experienced great things, but at the end of their life, they experience what many people seem to. They cannot remember those experiences due to an illness of the mind.

Everything is erased. What a sad outcome we have waiting for us at our eventual end.

This is why it is imperative for everyone to take photographs and record videos to be able to remember to your life. This should be important to everyone. It should be imperative to preserve the memory of experiences. If you have a record of things, you have done and seen, you can NEVER lose the memory. These records help you relive the moment.

So, while I wrote these stories, hopefully someone may read them and find them humorous, sad or they may not even like it at all. While I hope that this may get published at some point, the reality is, this may be simply just a collection of memories for me personally. I will be able to read this at my own eventual end of life and it will help me to remember all of the crazy things I have done. The great experiences I have had, and to know, even if I don't remember, that I did have a life, good and bad, at some point in time.